# FACING

THE SEARCH FOR COURAGE

# FEAR

Robert J. Furey, PhD

# FACING

## THE SEARCH FOR COURAGE

# FEAR

ALBA · HOUSE    NEW · YORK

SOCIETY OF ST. PAUL. 2187 VICTORY BLVD. STATEN ISLAND. NEW YORK 10314

*Library of Congress Cataloging-in-Publication Data*

Furey, Robert J.
      Facing fear : the search for courage / by Robert J. Furey.
          p.       cm.
      Includes bibliographical references.
      ISBN 0-8189-0589-1
      1. Fear.  2. Courage.   I. Title.
BF575.F2F87    1990
179'.6 — dc20                               90-40528
                                                    CIP

Designed, printed and bound in the United States of
America by the Fathers and Brothers of the
Society of St. Paul, 2187 Victory Boulevard,
Staten Island, New York 10314, as part of their
communications apostolate.

© *Copyright 1990 by the Society of St. Paul*

**Printing Information:**

Current Printing - first digit      2  3  4  5  6  7  8  9  10  11  12

Year of Current Printing - first year shown
                          1994     1995     1996     1997

# DEDICATION

*To*
*my parents,*
*Veronica and Robert, Sr.*
*and to*
*my daughter, Annie.*

# *Table of Contents*

# *Introduction*

What follows is a simple book about courage. No scholarly formulas or sophisticated schemes. Rather, we will remain as uncomplicated as possible. The reasons for this approach are not difficult to explain. First, people seem to speak the language of simplicity better than we do the language of complexity. Second, when we reach those points in our lives where we really need courage, seldom are we looking for intricate, mysterious philosophies. Instead, it is exactly at these times that we come to revere simplicity. Third, the paths to courage are themselves simple. Consequently, those comfortable with simplicity tend to have an easier time finding strength.

In the pages ahead there may be no point more profound than the one made by my seven-year-old son Shawn. I asked him recently for his thoughts on courage. After a moment of silence, he said quietly, "Some people have courage and they don't know it." Sometimes we have to find the courage we already possess. At other times we have to look elsewhere. The roads to courage, though often uncharted, are there for the traveling.

Just as there are many paths one can choose in life, there are many roads to courage. Ultimately, though, certain paths choose us. Whether we accept our callings depends on how much courage we have and whether or not we learn that, in the final analysis, it is the source of our callings that provides us with the courage to fulfill them.

We will begin our search in the realm usually described as "the psychological" and then move into the territory called "the spiritual." If we can face the anxiety that accompanies an open mind, we can learn and grow. If not, we can only agree or disagree. It is not the intention of this work to settle all uncertainty or remove all fear. This could only be achieved by numbing ourselves. Instead, we will be successful if we come closer to the force that enables us to walk through fear.

# FACING

### THE SEARCH FOR COURAGE

# FEAR

*Plunge boldly into the thick of life!*
Johann Wolfgang von Goethe

# CHAPTER I

## *Looking For Courage*

If there is one statement we could all utter with equal honesty, it might be: "It's not easy being me." It's a claim that seems to ring true whether spoken through tears, smirks or giggles, in good times or in bad.

Shakespeare advised that, above all else, "to thine own self be true." But he never said it would be easy. It takes courage, sometimes a lot of courage. Courage keeps you true to yourself. Your courage drives you to make your point, share the feeling, donate blood, take the exam, apologize, tell the joke, and admit you don't know. In short, courage is the energy that puts all other values into action.

Courage does not imply an absence of fear. Rather it insists you do what you believe is right *in spite* of your fear. Maybe John Wayne said it best when he described courage as "being scared to death — and saddling up anyway." It takes more than a horse to ride into the source of one's fears. It takes courage.

Although many have defined courage as a concept or an idea, I've never found these descriptions to be of much help. When we are scared, we don't usually need a theory. We need a push or a pull. More than anything, we need a *force* that moves us to do what we know is right. *Courage is this force.*

So we begin with this simple understanding: courage is a force, a force that puts our consciences and our values into action. And this leads to what may be the most important message of this book. *Courage is there for everyone, at all times.* This force does not discriminate. It makes itself available to all. How we tap this force will be discussed in the pages ahead.

~~ ~~ ~~

When I was a kid, I thought I owned the Atlantic Ocean. I grew up in Wildwood, one of the southernmost points on the New Jersey shore. Because Wildwood has the ocean on its east side, the bay on its west and inlets to the north and south, I'm one of the few native born Americans who can truly say they were raised on an island.

I lived a couple of hundred yards from the ocean. In Wildwood, every kid called the portion of the beach at the end of his street, "my beach." I guess I took things a step further and assumed that if it were "my beach," it must also be "my ocean." And ownership had its rewards. I could use the ocean without charge whenever I wanted. And, unlike the vacationers, I didn't have to leave when September came. Most importantly, the ocean would never hurt its owner. I never gave a second thought to sharks, jellyfish, crabs, stomach cramps, undertows or drowning. The water would always be safe.

Owning the ocean never burdened me with any responsibilities. It pretty much took care of cleaning itself. What the ocean couldn't do, the sea gulls seemed to do for it. These intriguing birds helped clean the beach and added sounds that completed the language of the seashore. But while I owned the ocean, I didn't understand its language.

Everything changed in the summer of my ninth year. While swimming in the ocean with a friend and his older sister, something completely unexpected occurred. I don't know if I stepped in a hole or got knocked down by a wave or underestimated the undertow, but I went under and could not get back to the surface. Almost immediately I knew I was in trouble. I wasn't a very good swimmer . . . probably because I didn't believe I would ever need to be. At one point I looked up and saw the sun beaming into the water. At that instant it occurred to me that I was going to die. The ocean was going to kill me and all I could think was, "It doesn't care! It doesn't care!"

I had reached the point where the pain begins to stop and resignation takes over. I felt certain that no one had seen me go under, so I had little hope. As I began to black out, however, I felt a hand on my arm. What seemed like the hand of God belonged to my friend's teenage sister. She pulled me back into the shallow water and to the surface. She never said a word to me and I'm not even sure if I ever thanked her. I struggled back toward the beach spitting out salt water and leaving a different ocean than the one I had entered.

For a while after that I didn't know how to approach the ocean. I felt betrayed, that somehow I had been lured into a dangerous trap. So I decided that, for the time being, I would stay out of the water.

Most confusing was that from the beach the ocean looked the same as before. The waves rolled toward the shore and the gulls circled above. But now the water was dangerous. There were sharks and sea monsters everywhere. The undertow was cruel and merciless. Still in all, from the beach the scene looked as it always had.

Certain experiences refuse to be forgotten. They seem to stay right in front of you until you make sense of them. It's like living on an island and being afraid of water. You have to somehow make things right.

Eventually I found my way back into the ocean. For the next few summers, though, I was too guarded to enjoy it. I stepped cautiously and never ventured far from shore. While I protected myself I watched with envy all the other swimmers reveling in the tide. I couldn't decide if I knew something they didn't or if they knew something of which I was unaware.

Sometime during adolescence the pieces of the puzzle began to fit. A Zen expression states: "When the mind is ready, a teacher appears." The teacher, it seems, need not be human. As I sat on the bulkhead one early August evening listening to the sounds of the surf and the sea gulls, a message came to me. Though I heard no voices in the literal sense, I felt the ocean making a simple statement: "Respect me!"

Suddenly things started making sense. There *was* danger in the water. But there was also vitality, beauty and exhilaration. I couldn't own the ocean, but I could befriend it. I learned to swim better. I began to respect the undertow. I then gradually became more spontaneous in the water, all the while appreciating its power, mystery and grandeur.

My arrogance led to trauma which resulted in fear. When my fear turned to respect I found contentment. I live in the Midwest now, and miss the ocean much as one would miss an old and faithful friend.

I sometimes think children know more about courage than anyone. They flock to heroes who fight evil and save the day.

In fact, fairy tales may be among our most sophisticated methods of teaching courage. "Jack in the Beanstalk," "Sleeping Beauty," "Cinderella," "Snow White," and "Hansel and Gretel" all teach children that no matter how bad things get, the situation can be changed. Although every parent tells these stories in a unique manner, the theme remains pretty consistent: Where there is courage, there comes magic. The courageous soul arrives at happy endings.

Renowned psychologist Bruno Bettelheim has demonstrated the importance of fairy tales in child development. He believes there exists a message inherent in these stories.

> This is exactly the message that fairy tales get across to the child in manifold form: that a struggle against severe difficulties in life is unavoidable, is an intrinsic part of human existence — but that if one does not shy away, but steadfastly meets unexpected and often unjust hardships, one masters all obstacles and at the end emerges victorious.[1]

Through the fairy tale, the original displeasure of anxiety turns into the great pleasure of anxiety successfully faced and mastered.[2] Thus children learn a simple, yet extremely important fact of life. When we encounter various monsters, dragons, evil giants, witches and wicked trolls in our life, our journey does not have to end.

As we age, we learn that these monsters take many forms. We can encounter rejection, despair, illness, injury, the threat of death, humiliation and many other kinds of pain. And unlike fairy tales, once we get beyond the first dragon, there may be many others. In real life, the journey never ends.

Also, as we grow older and wiser, we come to know that

we need not always kill the troll. Sometimes retreating makes more sense. But perhaps the most difficult lesson of all is the understanding that maybe the troll has a right to be there. Maybe he is not, in fact, an obstacle in our path but, rather, a very important part of our journey. How we handle each monster may determine the nature and condition of our next stretch of the road.

～～ ～～ ～～

Courage doesn't make things easier. It makes things possible! Courage does not imply an absence of fear. Instead it insists that we do what we believe is right *in spite* of our fear. Courage does not remove fear as much as it helps us act in the face of anxiety. In this sense, courage and cowardice have the same underlying feeling: Fear! Still, a clear difference exists. A coward's first priority is to remove the fear. A courageous soul's first priority, on the other hand, is to do what is right.

This drive to do what is right makes courage the motor that pushes all our values into action. Rollo May claims that courage "is not a virtue or value among other personal values like love and fidelity. It is the *foundation* that underlies and gives reality to all other virtues and personal values. Without courage our love pales into mere dependency. Without courage our fidelity becomes conformism."[3] It also seems difficult to conceive of honesty existing without courage.

In the world of values there are probably no teachers, only pupils. While trying to decide right from wrong we often face uncertainty along with the realization that others cannot decide for us. What I believe is right is not necessarily the same as what I know for sure. If we had the luxury of certainty, we wouldn't need courage. Gordon Allport once said, "We can be half sure and, at the same time, whole hearted." If we wait until we are absolutely sure about something before we act on it, we would be virtually paralyzed. Courage means acting on what we believe is right in spite of the uncertainty. Refusing to act on what we feel and think is right is what Confucius called "the worst cowardice."

Courage puts intention into action. But unlike fairy tales, the courageous act does not always lead to success. Heroes die in battle. Martyrs perish for their convictions. President John Kennedy's classic study, *Profiles in Courage*, details the bravery of several prominent American politicians. While these men demonstrated valor under intense pressure, their actions — for the most part — did not lead to happy endings. They took unpopular stands which, though admired by history, angered the voters of their day and (in many cases) ended their political careers.

Sometimes there are no apparent rewards for a courageous act. We can't always count on history to catch us in its lens and prove us correct. Sometimes an act that takes every ounce of our fortitude goes completely unnoticed or even brings ridicule. At these times our only reward comes from the knowledge that we have been true to ourselves and have acted in an honorable way. Whether or not this is enough reinforcement to continue acting courageously is up to each of us.

Doing what is right without thought of reward represents perhaps the finest achievement of human nature. Winston Churchill once suggested that without courage, all other virtues lose their meaning. Courage puts our best intentions, even the risky and unpopular ones, into action. Then, even in the face of criticism, cynicism or skepticism, we can live with ourselves knowing we stayed true to our values.

Courage doesn't always involve moving mountains. Somtimes it just means putting one foot in front of the other.

~~ ~~ ~~

Mark felt it was time to die. Although he had given the idea serious consideration in the past, he had reached the point where he could not see his life surviving the night.

Mark's father had been committed to a mental institution after years of drinking and violence that was eventually attributed to schizophrenia. Mark's family lived with the shame that accompanied his father's bizarre and dangerous public behavior. At age fifteen when his father was finally confined, Mark asked his mother if the family could change their name.

Mark began using drugs in his early teens and continued to do so up till that fateful night. A good looking young man, he dated many girls and had done well in school. He seemed to have all the social skills necessary to fit in, but inside himself he felt out of control.

Like many children of mentally ill parents, Mark feared his future. What may have been normal adolescent confusion was, Mark believed, a taste of the insanity sure to lie ahead. Seeing nothing but torment in the offing, at age seventeen he looked for a way out.

Several years earlier, Mark had acquired a .22 caliber handgun. Until this night, it had never been used. Hindsight suggests that it had always been intended for one thing. Now came its time to serve its purpose.

Alone in his room, Mark reached for the pistol. He had gotten this far several times before. He entered new territory, however, when he raised the gun to his head. He paused for a moment, then pulled the trigger.

He didn't know where he would be after it was over, but he never figured he'd be back in his room. The gun had misfired. This young man who considered himself the most unlucky kid in the world had just survived a deadly suicide attempt.

Still not ready to give up on giving up, Mark tried again. He checked the bullets and then shook the weapon. Convinced finally that the first miss was only a fluke, he once again pressed the barrel to his temple. Again he paused, and once more tripped the hammer.

Still no sound. Maybe, he frantically thought, there would be no way out. Desperately he changed the bullets and snapped the gun back together. Shaking the pistol as if to punish it, he then — for the final time — positioned it next to his head. No hesitation this time. He simply aimed and pulled the trigger.

It seems some lives are not for the taking. Three shots at point blank range, three misfires. Still not ready to look for alternatives, Mark shook the weapon violently between his face and his lap. Something had to happen. Something did. Without touching the trigger, the gun fired sending a bullet into Mark's thigh. Stunned and bleeding, he crawled up the stairs to his mother's bedroom.

When they arrived at the hospital, Mark denied a suicidal intent. Instead, he reported that he had been playing with the gun when it accidentally went off. Although the hospital staff had its doubts, they released him after a four-day stay. His mother, however, insisted he get counseling.

I met Mark seven days after the "accident." Even though he kicked and screamed about coming to see me, we soon developed a close relationship. Mark didn't want to admit it at first but he needed someone who would listen. A scared kid who didn't know who or how to ask for help, he had just had his only solution taken from him.

"How do you explain the three misfires?" I asked him.

"I have no idea," he replied with obvious bewilderment on his face. "I never gave much thought to the God business but I can't think of any other way to explain it." He now had a starry look about him.

The philosopher Nietzsche claimed that, "He who has found a *why* to live for can bear with almost any how." While Mark did not yet know the *why* to his life, he had become convinced that one existed. He now knew there was a reason the Grim Reaper refused to take him. Now he faced the difficult, yet tremendously healthy, task of finding the meaning of his life — a meaning he knew existed.

After that fateful night Mark no longer considered suicide an option. It's important to understand, though, that this was the only thing that changed that night. All his other problems remained. The family troubles, for instance, were waiting for him when he left the hospital. But this one change had a drastic impact on Mark. He now insisted upon *facing* what life had to offer. He stopped asking "if" he should live his life and began asking "how" he should live it.

Mark gave up the drugs, graduated from high school and found a job he liked. The last I heard from him he was doing well. With the determination to live came a courageousness that will, hopefully, live in him for the rest of his life. He will encounter other dragons and monsters as his journey continues. I like to think he will deal with each of them, in spite of his fear.

Later, we will discuss the sources of courage. We must note, however, that sometimes we cannot easily explain how people find their courage.

Perhaps the most important lesson about courage is that it exists, always. Courage is available to everyone, at any time in our lives. We can begin to develop it at any point. But it may not come cheap. It usually requires an effort, sometimes a very serious effort.

In order to become and then remain courageous, we need to do at least two things. We need to *recognize* courage and we need to *practice* courage.

### Recognizing Courage

Charles Kennedy once called courage "a peculiar kind of fear." This emphasizes the fact that fear accompanies courage. Courage can be hard to recognize because even when we use it we still feel scared. On occasion the fear becomes so intense that we move into numbness. People who have performed acts of bravery such as rescuing someone from a burning building sometimes report that they didn't feel the fear until the feat was over. While they engaged in their heroics, heroes frequently say they were just too focused on their mission to feel much of anything.

You can be terrified and yet be very courageous. You can use your guts while your stomach twists in knots. Even when your emotions seem to shut down you can find your fortitude. But in order to develop your courage, you must recognize it.

People who believe they are cowards tend to avoid situations that require courage. As a result, they rarely practice their courage. Courage, for better or worse, is a muscle that atrophies without exercise. People who know they have access to courage do not avoid challenges. They risk, dare and explore, all in an effort to do what they believe is right.

People who recognize their courage know they are capable of courage. This in turn generates even greater amounts of valor. Great acts of bravery usually catch our attention. It's the everyday courage that gets neglected. For example, it takes courage to walk away from the gossip that so often accompanies office politics. Walking away from a backbiting crowd can cause them to turn their venom toward you. This takes nerve. No one likes being criticized; we would rather be part of the group, the herd. Peer pressure can make us sheep. Rising above this pressure restores our humanity. Most of us, at some point, have the opportunity to know this triumph.

Caring for a baby, listening to the questions of an inquisitive four-year-old and introducing yourself to a stranger all require courage. So does asking for a raise, giving the toast at a wedding or eating that scary looking new dish your host prepared "just for you." There are no insignificant acts of courage.

I once heard someone say that the first step to learning French is to admit you don't know French. This being the case, you might think it would be easy getting started. But admitting we don't know something can be daring. It exposes us as less than all-knowing, which leaves us vulnerable to being criticized.

Scholars always have more questions. Every time we ask and explore we demonstrate our mettle. As Camelot deteriorated before his eyes, King Arthur returned to the forests of his youth to stir the memories of his mentor Merlin. In the midst of the woods he recalled this advice: "The best thing to do in times of despair is to *learn* something." Learning new skills and information can lead to solutions. Equally important, learning can restore our faith in our own courage.

Curiosity, which prompts us to explore the unknown, prods us to practice courage. Delving into the unknown is never easy; it arouses in us our most primitive fears.

Whenever we need to be reminded of how courageous we really are, we should *learn something new.*

Like curiosity, generosity seems to owe a debt of gratitude to courage. Psychologists have identified hundreds of fears or "phobias" but no one, to my knowledge, has coined a term for the all too common fear of generosity. Sometimes, in fact, it seems this phobia has become an epidemic. Maybe people fear that what they give away they may need later. Or perhaps contributing to a cause reveals too much about the giver. In any case, it seems clear that many folks would like to be generous but can't find the gumption to get started.

Even the good-natured humorist, Will Rogers, couldn't overlook the pervasive fear of generosity. "There ain't but one thing wrong with every one of us in the world, and that's selfishness." And when asked if he saw things getting better, Rogers shook his head and replied, "I doubt very much if civilization (so called) has helped generosity. I bet the old cave man would divide his raw meat with you a lot quicker than one of us would ask a down-and-outer to go in and have a meal with us. Those old boys and girls would rip off a wolf skin breech cloth and give you half of it quicker than a Ph.D. would slip you his umbrella."

I don't believe most selfish people want to be selfish. Instead, they simply lack the courage to live a generous life. For many, material things represent security; their loss or lack, the opposite. No one likes to feel insecure. Generosity takes courage. Every time you drop change into the March of Dimes canister you demonstrate your courage. Realize this! Your generosity demonstrates your courage.

Recognizing courage builds courage. Make a list of all the times that you can remember when you acted courageously. This may be difficult at first, but stay with it. Look for occasions when you were honest when honesty seemed threatening. Identify instances when remaining loyal to a friend cost you other social, political or business opportunities. Point out to yourself those situations where you followed your conscience even though you saw rewards for doing otherwise. If it helps, ask someone close to you for input on your list. We all need help at times in recognizing our courage.

If your list comes up short, don't give up. Everyone can develop courage. You start where you are right now. To build courage, you need to recognize courage. You also need to practice it.

### Practicing Courage

Courage is there for everyone. Some folks have an easier time reaching for it because they reach for it more often. Like all other values, courage grows and becomes more accessible each time we use it.

Shakespeare's advice deserves our consideration: "Assume the virtue, even if you have it not. For use almost can change the stamp of nature." Such a simple idea, an idea Benjamin Franklin put to use and included in his *Autobiography*. As a young man he made a list of all the personal qualities he believed worth acquiring. "I made a little book," Franklin wrote, "in which I allotted a page for each of the virtues. . . . I determined to give a week's strict attention to each."[4] This young printer from Philadelphia thus developed a therapeutic procedure as effective as any we have developed since. Unfortunately, this simple exercise has been overlooked by many of our modern healers and helpers.

If you want to develop a virtue, practice it. There are no effective shortcuts here. There is, however, an unfortunate misconception concerning the availability of instant bravery. A large portion of illicit drug users claim they take drugs because they feel drugs give them "guts." While "high," they can face and "deal with" things they believe they otherwise could not. At first glance, this might appear correct. A line of cocaine or a few shots of whiskey can help some people reveal their feelings, speak their minds and present themselves with more self-confidence. But the lie becomes obvious when you watch people try to recover from drug addiction.

Drugs don't provide courage — they mask fear. While using drugs, users don't have to face their fears. But in the process, their courage atrophies and they lose control. As the situation worsens, they feel incapable of tapping the force that keeps them true to themselves, true to the values that were once important to them. A kind of hopelessness sets in and their anxieties accumulate.

The downward spiral continues until their fears become so great that the drugs can no longer tame them. This place has a name: rock bottom. If ever a person needs courage, it's when they've hit rock bottom. But courage is something that they haven't tapped since their drug use began. As a result, many never leave rock bottom alive.

Fortunately, though, a number do manage to work their way back. But how? How does someone with virtually no courage left, begin to reconstruct an almost destroyed life? In short, in the beginning of their recovery, they must borrow the courage of others. As we will discuss in greater detail in the next chapter, we can lend courage to others in times of need. Once they are on their feet, however, they must begin building their own courage. Building one's courage becomes a crucial element in ongoing recovery.

Drugs and alcohol don't provide fortitude. Just ask

anyone who has ever been to rock bottom. You can't find "courage in a bottle" because this potion doesn't exist. We develop courage step by step and we can begin at any point in our lives.

Everyone has opportunities for practicing courage. Fear often points us towards these situations. Ask yourself, "When am I afraid to do what I believe is right?" Your answers will direct you to opportunities for courage and growth. Dag Hammarskjold once stated, "He who wills adventure will experience it — according to the measure of his courage." We could paraphrase Hammarskjold and note that he who wills *growth* will experience it — according to the measure of his courage. Every time you use your courage, you grow.

We walk a little stronger each time we walk through a fear. Fear may mean "danger ahead" but danger ahead doesn't always mean "stop." Sometimes, in order to be true to ourselves, we have to trespass through anxiety.

We all tap courage in our own ways. We choose our paths to the well. The more we use these paths, the greater our familiarity with them. The well is always full but it is not always easy to find. We mark our paths through repeated use. Without regular use, the grass returns and the paths disappear.

In order to find courage, we must enter into situations that call us to walk through our fears. With every courageous act we become more courageous.

Courage exists, always. We begin to tap it as we appreciate, recognize and practice it. Is it worth the effort? I believe so, but clearly this is a question you will have to answer for yourself. In order to help you reach your own conclusion, we will now consider two potentially devastating fears that each of us must face: the fear of people and the fear of life. Let's see if we can decide if it's worth walking through these fears.

*Courage is clearly a readiness*
*to risk self-humiliation.*
Nigel Dennis

*Approachable means vulnerable, woundable,*
*not made hard by a history of abuse, but like old*
*leather, made softer, more comfortable to be near.*
Hugh Prather — Note on Love and Courage

## CHAPTER II

# *Dealing With The Fear Of People*

" 'I don't care what people think' — that is the most dishonest sentence in the English language," writes Hugh Prather.[1] We'd like to believe we are insulated against the disapproval of others, but this doesn't seem to be the case. We can be hurt, sometimes deeply, by criticism. Deep inside we would prefer that *everyone* like and admire us. No one has yet, however, found a way to achieve this.

We get stuck in ruts by asking unproductive questions. One such query that can only lead to frustration is, "How can I get everyone to approve of everything I do?" We can spend our lives looking for the proper reply or we can realize that this question has no correct answer. Criticism is an inevitable, and potentially beneficial, part of life. We cannot avoid it. As soon as we accept this, our question becomes healthier. We then ask, "How can I deal with disapproval?" Since we cannot completely escape criticism, we can begin dealing with it by preparing for it.

You can't please all the people all the time. Just ask Theodor Seuss Geisel, a.k.a. Dr. Seuss. Dr. Seuss learned long ago not to be too concerned with pleasing everyone. "I once wrote a book on the ABCs," says the doctor. "It had twenty-six pages and we decided advance copies should be sent to twenty-six of the top educators in the country. They all wrote back and said it was the finest alphabet book ever written — with the exception of one page, which stank. *But they each named a different page!*"

The book, published without revisions, became a best seller. Dr. Seuss learned to "just ask myself, 'Will I like it?' "[2]

Sometimes the same act will make you a hero to some and a fool to others. Fifty-five-year-old Kurt, a construction worker, bemoans the fact that the fellows who drive the cement trucks don't like him.

"What's the trouble?" I ask.

"Well," sighs Kurt as he looks down at the floor, "you see, part of my job is to prepare the basements in new houses. I supervise the digging and the measurements and so on until it's time to pour the cement. Now usually the cement is poured first thing in the morning. But during the night frogs will come and settle into the freshly dug earth.

"The drivers don't like it a bit, but I won't let them pour until I chase all the frogs out of the area. You see, these guys are not choir boys and they'd just as soon pour their loads right on top of the frogs and then be on their way. In fact lately, with all the grief they've been giving me, I think a few of them would like to pour the cement on me."

Contrary to what these truckers may think, I suppose many would consider Kurt something of a hero. Maybe in time, the truckers will come to respect his convictions. For now, Kurt will have to face their scorn and follow his conscience against the backdrop of the rising sun in rural Missouri.

Fortunately for us all, people like Kurt can be found in many places. They balance vulnerability with determination. They can be hurt but they do not let the hurt block their path.

For several years I researched what psychologists call "eminent personalities." These "personalities" refer to people who have achieved greatness in a particular field. In short, I wanted to know, "What makes great people great? How do prominent scientists, athletes, statesmen, artists, businessmen, etc. reach such high levels of performance?"

Several theories already existed prior to my study but I wasn't comfortable with any of them. More than anything, I wanted to know if there is anything significant that all great people have in common. I reviewed the previous studies and read biography after biography. I began my research with several hypotheses but none of them proved true. My search for that common thread seemed, for a time, destined for failure. But in the face of defeat, I found the pot of gold. Only then did I realize the one thing all renowned people have in common: Critics!

I call it Furey's Simple Law of Greatness: "All great people have critics!" Furthermore, I believe this is the only remarkable experience shared by all eminent personalities. Being "accomplished" or "extraordinary" or even "saintly" does not mean "being loved by all." The lesson is clear. No one attains greatness without facing disapproval, sometimes a tremendous amount of disapproval.

While talent plays an important role in the development of eminence, it is not the most crucial factor in determining success. Many talented souls never use their gifts for fear of how they might be received. Some of the best writing in the world sits in old notebooks collecting dust because its authors dread the possible consequences of public scrutiny. The same is assuredly true for musical masterpieces and scientific breakthroughs. What we have hidden is so much more than what we share because if we share of ourselves — be it in the form of an idea, piece of art, or whatever — we can be criticized and, if we allow it, shamed.

Some people look to perfection as a form of protection. "If I am perfect," they reason, "I cannot possibly be criticized." So they restrict themselves to small arenas where the outcomes are predictable and the audience remains satisfied or indifferent. No risks, no daring. They resist any force that might lead them into new territories. Fresh scenarios call for new ideas and behaviors. New endeavors frequently invite mistakes. Mistakes, in turn, can lead to disapproval. Each of us has to decide if it's worth the risk.

One of the most important points in human development arrives when one learns how to deal effectively with critics. At this milestone one comes to understand that criticism has no more power than any other communication. Though it may contain information worthy of consideration, criticism does not (by itself) have the power to force a retreat. But we can let it.

In workshops on self-esteem, I ask participants to tell me how many compliments it takes to help them get over a single criticism. I ask them to envision this: "During the course of a single day, ten people compliment you on something important to you (e.g., your work, appearance, wit, etc.) and one person criticizes you on one of the same things.

Has this been a good day for your self-esteem?" Generally the results are pretty clear. We tend to give more credence to negative remarks aimed at us.

Even the healthiest among us have self-doubts. We're not everything we can imagine; we couldn't possibly be. Much of the region we refer to as "deep down inside" questions our adequacy in matters important to us. This isn't a flaw. It just seems to be the way we are constructed. But the criticism hurts because it appears that the critic is the one who has the ability to look deep inside and see the real you. He touches the part òf you that has the doubts about your ability, competence or attractiveness. The critic, it seems, is the one who really knows.

The critic represents the adult version of the bogeyman. In and of itself, it has no power. We can, however, give it clout — sometimes a lot of clout. Just as the bogeyman kept us out of the attic, the critic can, if we let him, keep us from climbing more significant ladders.

It might help to know the kinds of criticism others have faced. For instance, when Thomas Edison was a child, the headmaster of his school told him that he "would never make a success of anything." Likewise, a teacher once told Albert Einstein, "You will never amount to anything."

A newspaper editor once told a young struggling artist named Walt Disney that he had no artistic talent. And back in 1889, the *San Francisco Examiner* sent a rejection letter to Rudyard Kipling saying, "I'm sorry, Mr. Kipling, but you just don't know how to use the English language."

During her time, the *Atlantic Monthly* wrote of Emily Dickinson, "An eccentric, dreamy, half-educated recluse in an out-of-the-way New England village — or anywhere else — cannot with impunity set at defiance the laws of gravitation and grammar. . . . Oblivion lingers in the immediate neighborhood."[3] One hundred years have passed without the predicted "oblivion."

Walt Whitman, one of America's greatest poets, was the target of much ridicule during his lifetime. One review in *The London Critic*, for example, stated confidently that "Whitman is as unacquainted with art as a hog is with mathematics."[4]

Fortunately for us all, Edison, Disney, Einstein, Dickinson, Kipling and Whitman all kept producing. They continued in the face of discouragement. But what of all those who did not? What of all those "unknowns" that should have been known but whose voices fell silent after being discouraged? Herman Melville, for instance, now recognized as a literary genius, was criticized so harshly in his day that he stopped writing for nearly forty years.[5] Who knows the treasures lost?

We have to· learn to live with some disapproval. Otherwise we will live our lives solely for the purpose of endearing ourselves to critics. Popular American author Louis L'Amour once advised his fellow writers: "In the first place I do not believe writers should read reviews of their own books, and I do not. If one is not careful one is soon writing to please reviewers and not their audience or themselves."[6] In other words, don't give faultfinders your undivided attention. Instead, learn as much as you can and then get back to work. "Listen carefully to first criticisms of your work," suggested Jean Cocteau. "Note just what it is about your work that critics don't like — then cultivate it. That's the part of your work that's individual and worth keeping."[7] Is it a coincidence that all great people have critics? Maybe the mission of the critic is to keep things from changing. Perhaps talent threatens the status quo.

All people can be great people. In order to fulfill our potential, however, we must deal with the fear of disapproval. Never let nay sayers have the only word. Better to absorb the words of Neil Simon, spoken during a commencement address:

> Don't listen to those who say, "It's not done that way." Maybe it's not, but maybe you will. Don't listen to those who say, "You're taking too big a chance." Michelangelo would have painted the Sistine floor, and it would surely be rubbed out by today. Most importantly, don't listen when the little voice of fear inside of you rears its ugly head and says, "They're all smarter than you out there. They're more talented, they're taller, blonder, prettier, luckier and have connections. . . ." I firmly believe that if you follow a path that interests you, not to the exclusion of love, sensitivity, and cooperation with others, but with the strength and conviction that you can move others by your own efforts, and do not make success or failure the criteria by which you live, the chances are you'll be a person worthy of your own respect.[8]

If you ignore criticism completely, you may miss some valuable lessons. Constructive criticism — criticism delivered in a respectful manner intended to help — can, of course, be very beneficial. But so too can the caustic variety based on ignorance and vindictiveness. Destructive criticism might have been what Nietzsche had in mind when he said, "That which does not kill me, makes me stronger." Even an insult can provide an education. It all depends on what you do with it.

We like to think that if we had been there as the naked king paraded by, we too would have courageously exclaimed,

"The emperor has no clothes!" Maybe so. Maybe not. It's hard to know. We like to think we have the stuff heroes are made of, but we don't like taking the risks necessary to find out.

We live in a world where we can all be heroes, although not everyone's heroism will be recognized by the crowds. The opportunities are endless if we are willing to face the fear and understand the true nature of heroism. Heroism describes the triumph of virtue over adversity. I glimpsed such a triumph recently while on a picnic in Bloomington, Illinois. While there, I saw a mother push her wheelchair-bound son through the park. As they traveled, the young man, who appeared to be in his late teens and suffering from cerebral palsy, leaned over the side of his chair and took in the people and events that surrounded him.

Mother's sturdy legs kept a steady pace as she accommodated the hills and turns. All the while she maintained a conversation with her young passenger. I wondered what they talked about. They seemed familiar with their journey, as if this may have been an important part of their daily routine. They weren't proud. But they weren't ashamed either. They personified both tragedy and triumph. They probably never realized they were heroes. If asked, I bet the mother would deny the great courage she displays every day. She would probably tell us she is only doing what she can to help her son.

But, oh, what courage!

Some heroes care for the less fortunate. Others, like the emperor's young enlightener, speak the views of the frightened and the silent. Different kinds of risks, but risks nonetheless. They have a common thread. All acts of courage communicate the same message: "This is me!" Every act of courage makes an important statement about you. The soldier who jumps on the grenade to save his buddies makes a powerful statement. So too does the person who begins volunteer work at the local hospital. The risks are very different but the message remains the same: "This is me!"

With exposure comes vulnerability. By exposing your beliefs and convictions you open yourself up for possible ridicule and rejection. Yet without this self-disclosure and vulnerability neither honesty nor intimacy would be possible. Psychologist Charles Gourgey explains that we must have "the willingness to be embarrassed." This is "the only medicine that can heal a pretender. If we are pretending, we are trying to preserve an image of ourselves that we know is false. If we are willing to be embarrassed, we become free of the tyranny of this false self-image."[9]

If I somehow communicate "This is me!" I may wind up mortified. If I refuse to expose the real me, however, I will experience boredom, guilt and loneliness. So what do we do? If we want to thrive, we have to risk the humiliation. And if the humiliations come, we must be willing to face them again. Once you have walked through the fear of being embarrassed, you are well on your way to making your mark on the world.

The fear of people is quite common. One name for this condition is shyness. Social psychologist Philip Zimbardo, widely recognized as the world's leading authority on shyness, tells us that "to be shy is to be afraid of people, especially people who for some reason are emotionally threatening: strangers because of their novelty and uncertainty, authorities who wield power, members of the opposite sex who represent potential intimate encounters."[10] If strangers, authority figures and members of the opposite sex can all be threatening, then there certainly is a lot to fear. Beyond this, we do not seem to have adequate guidelines on how to act in some of the most common situations. For instance, if you watch any group of people long enough you will probably notice that most individuals simply don't know, or haven't made up their minds, whether or not they should say hello to a stranger. And how friendly is *too* friendly?

We don't have exact directives on how to relate to others. What's funny to one may be offensive to another. What one might consider "being too forward," another might consider meek. We can develop our sensitivity and tact but we never erase the risk altogether. In relationships we can be hurt. Each of us must ask ourselves, "Are they worth it?"

Research clearly demonstrates that shyness can be a terrible cross to bear. Retreating from the social world to avoid danger does not provide a happy refuge. It merely creates a prison of loneliness and missed opportunities.

Shy people find little consolation in the fact that many people share their affliction. After interviewing almost five thousand people, Dr. Zimbardo reached the following conclusion.

> The most basic finding of our research establishes that shyness is common, widespread, and universal. More than eighty percent of those questioned reported that they were *shy at some point in their lives*, either now, in the past, or always. Of these, over forty percent considered themselves *presently shy* — that means four out of every ten people you meet, or eighty-four million Americans![11]

Having established the extent of the problem, we are left to ponder its consequences. As a graduate school instructor, I am constantly reminded of how the fear of people affects us. Typically, my courses end with students submitting a research paper as the final requirement prior to receiving their grade. Each semester I usually find at least several students who sit silently through the course only to perform brilliantly on exams and written assignments — students who not only report back what they have been given, but who analyze, synthesize and add magnificent, creative insights of their own. And each semester I shake my head and wonder how much more exciting the class would have been, for all, if I could have gotten these great minds to share themselves.

More disheartening, I sometimes worry about what will happen to these silent scholars after graduation. What happens when no one is there to insist they "hand in" their views? Too often great minds have weak voices. If we could get them to speak up we would all be richer.

It seems folks can be intimidated by recognition and acclaim. An art dealer once told me, "It's hard to explain, but so often you will see an artist struggle, struggle, struggle without any success. All the while sticking with it, producing a particular style of art. Then when he starts to get noticed and his pieces start to sell, he will change his style . . . sometimes completely. It's an amazing thing, but you see it all the time." Amazing and unfortunate.

Some people fear their gifts. A talent will get you recognized. It may also get you appreciated. Furthermore, it may incite envy. In all cases, however, a special skill will single you out as an individual, pull you out of the anonymity that accompanies life in the herd. Being unique can provoke anxiety. Yet if we shall be true to ourselves we have to walk through the fear. Gifts scream to be opened. They contribute to our calling. They help point us in the right direction. Even when we follow a correct path, we encounter fear.

Deep inside we all know we need other people. Because we need them so much, it can be frightening to risk their disapproval. The individual who drops a facade may lose some so-called friends. But in time, if she has the courage to stay honest, she will end up with real friends. In order to survive the vulnerability that comes with honest self- disclosure it can help to hold on to the simple fact that there are many many good people out there.

Not all dogs bite.

Intimacy involves at least two types of risk, exposing one's self and then accepting the individuality of another. It sounds easy enough. Still, both of these can be frightening. Intimacy requires a great deal of self-disclosure. These are the special relationships where you share important things — things that, when expressed, make you feel vulnerable.

Rollo May believes that one of the special feelings we deny expression is our appreciation of beauty.

> . . . like the majority of people in our western culture, we suppress our feelings of beauty; we are shy about them; they are too personal, too soul baring. We talk about "the view," anything to avoid the personal statement. And if we do let out such feelings we apologize for them. . . .[12]

Interestingly enough, one of the most revealing statements we can make about ourselves involves our perception of beauty. We say a lot about ourselves when we point out the things we feel are beautiful. And we learn much about others when they reveal to us things they regard as magnificent.

But just as sharing ourselves can be difficult, so too can receiving personal thoughts from those in our lives. When we hear things that remind us that the people close to us are truly unique we are also reminded that we are, to some extent, "different."

Some time ago at a wedding reception a friend of mine worked up the nerve to ask me something that seemed to have been on his mind for some time. Although still a bachelor, Matt had been dating the same woman — Linda — for over five years. With a drink in his hand and a bit of the tipsy in his walk, he proceeded to tell me how he wanted to get married but that he worried about Linda. Specifically, he had concerns about her mental health.

"What do you mean?" I asked, though a bit reluctant to delve into this.

"Well," he replied as he scanned for eavesdroppers, "whenever she travels anywhere for an overnight stay, she has to bring along her own pillow. Her mother gave it to her a long time ago and she won't go anywhere without it."

Having said this, he looked at me with a facial expression that seemed to say, "Can you believe it?!"

I waited a few seconds assuming there must be more to it. He didn't offer any additional information, though. Instead he made it clear he needed a response or, as he said, "a professional opinion."

I know better than to give advice at weddings, but I felt compelled to respond.

"It sounds like a quirk, Matt."

"What?" he asked, his confusion apparent.

"A *quirk*. We all have them. It's just the way we're built."

Whatever answer he had prepared himself for, it wasn't this one. Bewilderment written all over his face, he paused, stuttered and then changed the subject. (Matt and Linda married a year later.)

The paradox of mental health lies in the fact that mental health comes only to those who accept their fair share of craziness. We all have quirks, idiosyncrasies and amusing fantasies. When we get close to someone, we enter their private terrain. If you expect to find things just as they are in your unique world, you will be disappointed, confused and afraid. When we understand that each person has a special set of talents, flaws, gifts and peculiarities, intimacy becomes an adventure.

Soldiers in dangerous combat situations need all the courage they can muster. So we learn a lot about courage by studying how people fare in battle.

General George Patton claimed that there are "no atheists in foxholes," suggesting that when their lives are on the line, combat soldiers look to God for support. Even those warriors who might have denied His existence the day before, while safe and warm back at the base, find faith when their fear and uncertainty rise. We can learn in the face of death. Perhaps, as Leo Buscaglia says, "Death is the greatest of life's teachers."

Besides prayer, there exists a second procedure to help troops deal with fear. Prior to combat, officers will take roll call. They call the name of each man, who responds immediately with a resounding reply. Every name called reminds each soldier that he is not alone. Roll call, then, serves as a reminder that "we are all in this together," an attitude that lifts morale and strengthens courage.

The lesson could not be simpler: we receive courage from others and we can provide courage to others. A fear of people, consequently, begins a vicious downward spiral. If we fear people, we distance ourselves from a major source of the courage we seek. The more we distance ourselves from them, the less we are likely to see, hear or feel their encouragement and our fear deepens. Fear of people begets fear of people.

Those caught in it must find a way to reverse the spiral. They must make a conscious effort to look for someone they feel safe with. That someone may be a professional counselor or a member of the clergy. It could also be a neighbor. Good, caring, understanding people are everywhere but we have to be willing to make contact with them.

It can be scary getting close to someone or asking someone for help . . . so scary that we can focus solely on the dangers and lose sight of the potential rewards. Sometimes, perhaps often, we have to take the first step by ourselves. Once contact is made, however, good relationships produce courage.

The word "courage" comes from the Latin word *cor* which means "heart." To encourage is to hearten. Relationships that do not support and inspire your efforts to be true to yourself are not healthy relationships. Instead of encouraging, they discourage. In other words, they take the heart right out of you.

These discouraging relationships can be very problematic. At first glance one might suggest that the best thing to do would be to end an unhealthy relationship like this and move along. And if the relationship cannot be changed, then this advice has merit. Unfortunately, when persons have been discouraged long enough, they can have a difficult time' finding the "heart" or the "guts" to end the association. In encouraging relationships, people grow together. In discouraging relationships, individuals have a tendency to get stuck in stagnating environments. But it takes courage to improve one's situation in life and courage is the thing they feel has been taken from them.

One of the clearest signs of discouragement occurs

when one gives up on other people. Discouraged souls seem to think, "They are all alike," and see little hope of finding a relationship that can provide the things they need to thrive. In short, severely discouraged souls give up on the hope of ever being encouraged. They lose faith in the simple fact that there are good people out there. If this faith can be restored, wonderful changes begin.

Psychologist Lewis M. Andrews makes the point that "we have to remember that the most important thing we can give a floundering person is not our enlightened manipulation but our courage."[13] We can offer courage by way of a hug, a handshake, a shoulder to cry on, a kind word, a small gift or even a bit of humor. We can sometimes share courage by simply "being there" for a person in need. Probably the best advice on how to offer courage to someone is to *keep it simple*. No one arrives at courage through a complicated formula.

I've been reminded of this point in so many ways. Most recently, I encountered it again while doing a workshop at Scott Air Force Base in Illinois. My presentation was on "Fatherhood" and a crowd of forty or so officers gathered to address issues that frequently arise in military families. Toward the end of our time together, I asked the men how many of them had pictures of their families sitting on their desks. Almost to a man they immediately raised their hands. I then asked them, "Why?" They began rattling off answers. The first few responses indicated that the portraits helped remind them why they were doing what they were doing. When work became difficult, the pictures served to remind them why they were there. A few of the participants then suggested that the pictures helped them keep their "priorities in order."

Then came a statement that grabbed the entire audience. One of the officers, after patiently waiting his turn to speak, said simply, "It gives me courage." Everyone nodded in unison. No more responses were offered or needed. The group had clearly found their answer.

As I left the base, this point stayed with me. A soldier in military fatigues with a gun, radio and a German shepherd patrolled the gate as I departed. He reminded me of the dangers these men have faced including combat missions, test flights, and the kinds of peril that require the services of armed guards and attack dogs.

Family portraits, a simple source of spirit.

People provide courage. In order to find courage, we have to find encouragement. We begin by asking ourselves, "Who encourages me? Which of my relationships seem to instill in me a sense of conviction?" If you consider the questions seriously, your answers may be surprising, even humbling. It is not uncommon for adults to realize that on occasion they still need their parents to help them find courage. Or maybe a grandparent. Or even a child. We need to develop encouraging relationships. We need to make this a deliberate choice.

My young friend Steven has muscular dystrophy. When I first met him he was nineteen years old. Although still hoping for a cure, he knew he was running out of time. His muscles were failing him at a steady pace and as time passed his freedom waned. When I first met Steven he was also very depressed. He saw no future for himself, only a continued deterioration of body and spirit. Confined to a wheelchair since age eight, he now had only minimal strength in his neck and hands. His facial movements were appropriate, however, and his mind functioned as well as ever. A healthy mind to observe and ponder his condition.

Steven did not feel courageous. He laughed the time he told me how people called him courageous. "But that's just because people call all disabled people courageous," he said in a voice that tried not to carry too much cynicism.

"What does encourage you?" I asked.

"Nothing, I guess," he whispered.

"Nothing at all?" I insisted.

"Well, people try . . . but it doesn't really help. People say they admire me for going to college and I think a lot of people go out of their way to compliment me and be kind. And I *am* grateful. But I'm missing something."

As Steven spoke it occurred to me how difficult it can be to encourage people in certain situations. Our conversation ended with Steven apparently more depressed than before. As his electric wheelchair carried him away, I wondered who, if anyone, could help him.

Several days later, Steven returned with the answer.

"Hey, Rob, remember the other day when you asked me who or what encourages me?"

"Yeah, I do," I replied with enthusiastic curiosity.

"Well, I do have something . . . the *telethon!*"

"What?"

"The telethon, the Jerry Lewis Labor Day Telethon for Muscular Dystrophy. I have the telethon. It gets me through the year. In fact, there are times when I think that if I can make it to Labor Day, I'll be O.K."

As Steven spoke, I heard a sense of conviction, something I had not heard before. But in spite of the strength I was hearing, I knew the annual telethon was not enough for Steven. I had seen the depths of his depression and I knew he needed at least a little more.

"Steve, I have an idea. Why don't you write a letter to Jerry Lewis and tell him what you just told me?" But before I could say another word, I saw the fear in his face.

"But I don't have his address."

"I'll get it for you."

"Do you really think I should?"

"Yeah, I do."

It took five months of pushing and pestering until he finally wrote the letter. Steven saw himself as a frail, inadequate young man whose words might disappoint his hero. Although filled with emotion, he had a very difficult time articulating his feelings. When he finished his letter however, it was beautiful. His feelings — perhaps for the first time — found words in this honest, moving expression of gratitude.

Within two weeks came a reply from Jerry Lewis, a message that had more impact on Steven than I could have ever imagined. In it Steven found hope, love and *encouragement*. Now he had something to have and hold. The letter became a permanent part of his wheelchair. The two hands that could barely turn a page opened and read the words over and over and over again, each time restoring a little more life to his spirit.

Not long after receiving the letter, Steven decided to go on an overnight retreat with Handicaps Encounter Christ (HEC). Before a year had passed, he had gone to two more and he told me how much they were helping. He said he had found support and a renewed faith in God and that he planned to attend as many HEC retreats as he could.

His health is not improving. A cure, if there is to be one for Steven, will have to come soon. His growing spirit may not be able to sustain his weakening body much longer. These days he is, however, stronger. He found encouragement and now he encourages others in similar situations. Not a hero, rather a young man with the spirit to transcend adversity without losing touch with who he is or what he faces.

The moral to Steven's story: Look for the people who can provide you with courage and then let them touch you.

P.S. Thank you, Jerry Lewis.

~~  ~~  ~~

If social scientists could have one question answered once and for all, I believe the question most would want asked is, "What causes people to help other people?" In other words, what makes people kind? Hopefully, the perfect answer would also include a discussion of what *keeps* people from helping.

Since I don't have an answer machine, I have to draw my own conclusions. I believe most people want to be good, caring human beings. And if we could be compassionate without risking anything, I bet we'd be the kindest folks who ever lived. It's the risking that gets in the way. Kindness is a form of self-expression that can leave us very vulnerable. Few things hurt more than being rejected or ridiculed after offering to help someone. Then there is the possibility of being ineffective in our efforts to assist. Even though the likelihood of these disasters may be minimal, the possibility feeds the fear. And the fear can squelch the kindness.

I used to live in south St. Louis near the Missouri School for the Blind. Just about every day, students from the school would walk through the neighborhood. One of the things that caught my attention was the fact that they didn't use dogs to guide them. Instead, they depended on long white canes.

They had trouble, however, crossing the streets where traffic could get heavy at any time. Sometimes the students would wait on the corners, almost motionless. Being new to the area, and having no experience with the blind, I didn't know what to do. I was too cowardly to ask them if they needed help. So, for a time, I just watched.

Sometimes they traveled in pairs, but usually these young adults were alone. If enough time passed, and no one came to help, they would slowly move out into the street and then quickly cross until their canes touched safely on the opposite curb. Once on the pavement they could advance to the next corner where the procedure repeated itself. And each time I saw it I was reminded of their courage and my cowardice.

I knew what was right. I should have helped them. But it did, I confess, take a while. I saw a young woman almost get run over before I began to act on what I knew was right. The first blind person I walked across the intersection gave me a simple, sincere, "Thank you." I, in turn, wanted to thank her but I didn't think she would understand.

From that point on, I looked for the blind people. I felt good helping them, that somehow I was making a difference. With each soul I escorted across the road, I felt a little stronger.

More recently, I had a similar experience in a post office in Boston. As I waited in line talking to a friend, a young blind man walked in. He entered the lobby but stopped after one or two steps. He pulled his cane close to him and stood there silently. I knew he needed help but I waited a minute to observe the reactions of others. Not only did no one assist him, it seemed they were pretending not to see him. I walked over and escorted him to the clerk. People watched. He thanked me. I felt useful.

I guess wherever you go you can run into people afraid of the blind.

"I don't want to get involved," often means, "I'm afraid."

~ ~ ~

So why do people help other people? Many social scientists will tell you that altruism will occur when it is self-serving. For instance, John will help Jane only if John receives a reward for doing so. Perhaps he hopes to achieve recognition or the respect and appreciation of others. Maybe his action causes him to feel needed or useful. In any case, the love of self underlies what appears to be a selfless act.

Many of us resist this interpretation. We choose to believe, perhaps correctly, that one can sacrifice for the love of *others* and that this is why we act altruistically. It can seem as if the argument is two-sided. One side suggests that kindness is rooted in the love of self. The other side claims that the love of others leads to altruism. But there exists a third position, one that insists that kindness and courage are founded in the love of self *and* the love of others.

John Kennedy's *Profiles in Courage* profiled statesmen who acted quite courageously in their efforts to serve the people. In his conclusion, Kennedy sought to explain the origin of their courage. Why did these statesmen risk so much in order to do what they believed right?

> It was not because they "loved the public better than themselves." On the contrary, it was precisely because they did *love themselves* — because each one's need to maintain his own respect for himself was more important to him than his popularity with others — because his desire to win or maintain a reputation for integrity and

courage was stronger than his desire to maintain his office — because his conscience, his personal standard of ethics, his integrity or morality, call it what you will — was stronger than the pressures of public disapproval. . . . And it is when his regard for himself is so high that his own self-respect demands he follow the path of courage and conscience that all benefit.[14]

Self-respect means staying true to your beliefs in spite of the consequences. People who consistently demonstrate altruistic behavior possess at least two important characteristics. First, their ethical code includes a belief that one has an obligation to help others. This belief clearly reflects a *love of others*. Second, they maintain a commitment to their values. They *love themselves* enough to express their convictions and this makes them feel good.

Kindness owes its existence to the love of self and the love of others.

One of the best ways to develop your self-esteem is to work on increasing someone else's. By building someone else's confidence, we find our own gaining strength.

A simple method for lifting your self-esteem and your courage is the "three compliments a day" approach. Make a promise to yourself that each day you will look for at least three opportunities to compliment or encourage someone. The praise, of course, must be sincere. This means, if they are not obvious, you must look for qualities genuinely worth your admiration, then express your respect. Let others know you appreciate them. Generally people will not bite while receiving sincere applause and you will notice a good feeling within yourself. It's a small yet very beneficial risk.

The expression of praise, like the expression of gratitude, can be difficult. Fortunately, it is something that can develop with practice. Start small if you like. But remember: three compliments each day.

~~ ~~ ~~

Talking out a fear with someone special can build courage. I'm not sure why it works this way, but I know it is true. Talking out a fear with a friend seems to create the feeling: "I'm not alone." For the most part, we face fear better in groups. If we fear other people, and hence isolate ourselves, all our other fears multiply.

We need to understand this simple fact: *We all get scared sometimes.* We all need other people. No one is so superior as to be immune to this fact. It's easy to be intimidated by others if we attribute superhuman powers to them. Don't be misled; everyone gets scared. People become less frightening when we understand this.

~~ ~~ ~~

Loving parents encourage their children to try. Effective teachers encourage students to explore the unknown and learn. The best coaches encourage athletes to push themselves to reach their potential. Good friends encourage friends whenever they get the chance.

In Chapter Three we will deal with the fear of life. Conquering the fear of life, however, begins by overcoming the fear of people. We fear less when we have healthy, supportive, encouraging relationships. We need to look for and build such relationships for ourselves and provide these relationships to others. Only then are we ready to take on life.

*The tragedy of life is not how much
we suffer, but how much we miss.*
Thomas Carlyle

*Have the nerve to go into unexplored territory.
Be brave enough to live life creatively.
The creative is the place where no one else has ever
been. . . . What you'll discover will be wonderful.
What you'll discover will be yourself.*
Alan Alda

## CHAPTER III

# *Confronting The Fear Of Life*

"Just lately," writes Jean-Louis Servan-Schreiber, "after her son had committed suicide, one of my friends found the note he had left behind. 'Mother, you didn't tell me it takes courage to live.' "[1] A young man ends his life because he cannot face the fears that confront him. And a mother survives to anguish over the question, "What could I have done?"

How does one teach another about fear? Can we ever be fully prepared to deal with it before we encounter it? Probably not. If we could, there would be no fear.

Someone once noted that experience is the cruelest

instructor; it gives the test before it teaches the lesson. Maybe we don't realize our need for courage until we find ourselves scared. It certainly does take courage to live. This seems to be one of life's clearest messages. To those who do not learn this lesson, life seems incomprehensible and overwhelming. Everyone needs courage in order to face life.

I suspect that anyone who has read this far understands the need for courage. Furthermore, I believe that anyone who can recognize fear will realize they have experienced it. Fear is a universal experience. It can be denied, but it cannot be avoided.

Erich Fromm claimed that "thinking man is by necessity uncertain. Free man is by necessity insecure." Freedom and consciousness create a certain amount of anxiety. In other words, life produces fear. As we have discussed, most journeys have dragons. A wonderful Zen expression reminds us, "The obstacle is part of the path." The dangers we face produce the lessons we learn.

In spite of the obstacles, we may need to continue on the path. When we walk through a fear, we walk to courage. So we must deal with the trolls before we move on. French novelist Marcel Proust came to this conclusion: "We are healed of suffering only by experiencing it to the full." Similarly, we develop courage by experiencing fear to the full.

If that young man could have held on in spite of his fear, he may have found courage. It seems he did not understand this. Unfortunately, a parent cannot simply hand this lesson to a child. Life teaches.

In the journey of life there are no travel agents. You don't know for sure what you'll find until you get "there." In spite of the uncertainty, we seem designed to keep moving and growing, heading in some direction beyond the present.

Raymond Lindquist defined courage as "the power to let go of the familiar." We are explorers and discoverers by nature. Nothing can change this. We can deny our curiosities and pretend not to feel the push into the new. In so doing, however, we lose touch with ourselves. We lose our life force when we deny the gift of curiosity.

It has been said that, "It's better to be safe than sorry," and, for better or for worse, this has become a respected slogan for guiding behavior. Now I don't know who coined this phrase, but I'm willing to bet we have taken it out of context.

I won't argue that people prefer safety to sorrow — I certainly do. But is it always better to be safe than daring? Is it always preferable to be secure than to be vibrant and enthusiastic? Safety does not completely protect us from sorrow. And safety (in the short run) can lead to sorrow (in the long run). We ultimately miss the things we protect ourselves from.

The interesting fact is that we probably fear more things from our imaginations than things rooted in reality. For instance, most psychological surveys dealing with fears or "phobias" have reached similar conclusions. When asked to identify their greatest fear, one of the most common responses among adults is the fear of public speaking. It's remarkable that even people who never do public speaking will list this as their greatest fear.

When asked why they fear speaking before a crowd, adults say some curious things. "I'm afraid I'll go completely blank and look like a fool." "Because all the people might walk out on me." "I'm afraid that everyone in the audience will know more than me about the topic I'm discussing." "I'll have a complete and total mental breakdown in front of all those people." "It scares me that I could be up there exposing myself in front of the world and then feel rejected and humiliated."

I've been to, at least, hundreds of presentations and I've never seen any of these "what ifs" materialize. I know the fear though. I've had all these same thoughts at one time or another. It seems that even if we have not lived the worst, we can imagine the worst. And even if we've never seen *anyone* live out our nightmares, we can still imagine them coming true.

If we look closely, a certain irony emerges. The fear of public speaking may produce some of the best public speakers. According to his wife Betty, Will Rogers (the most popular speaker and humorist of his time) was terrified each time he addressed a group. Even after much experience and success he never lost the fear.

Psychologists have known for years that a certain amount of anxiety contributes to creativity and performance. Beyond this, it seems that the fear also prevents one from taking an audience for granted (the worst of all offenses). An anxious performer may become the most prepared performer.

But the real reason I suspect that the fear leads to a high quality performance relates to the fact that people revel in the conquest of fright. Remember, when you walk through a fear, you walk to courage. Speakers who survive the dread and find themselves at the podium can find terror turning to ecstasy. The "rush" then begins and wonderful performances unfold.

Being quite a fan of Will Rogers, and a collector of Rogers memorabilia, I have listened to many hours of his taped broadcasts. While listening, I never hear a frightened man. Rather, I hear someone charged with energy and delighted to be — at least for a while — on the other side of scared.

No, there are no travel agents for life's journey and this can be scary. Still, at each successive destination, we find the energy and the ecstasy to continue.

We all have our own maps to courage. The maps need updating as we age and find new sources of gumption. The more acquainted we are with our maps, the less we actually need them. Even so, it's important we not lose our directions; we're only human and humans forget things. We can forget how to find courage.

Most maps to courage are mental maps. Rarely discussed, we keep them safely and silently within. While all goes well, these directions seem to remain in the unconscious. Consequently, as long as we have the courage to live our values, we may not even be aware that such maps exist. When a crisis arises, however, and the map cannot be found, the conscious mind clamors for the map. In other words, when you face a situation that requires more courage than seems available to you, your conscious mind insists that your unconscious either find or update your map to courage.

Crises like this can be very distressing. You face a condition without the courage to deal with it. Your mind then starts digging for your map, a map you may never before realized even existed. And once you find the directions, they may only give you a portion of the information you need. They may only tell you where you found courage *in the past.* Your new crisis may require a new source of courage.

For example, let's consider the crisis of serious illness. Suddenly the patient learns that life may not last as long as he had hoped, that maybe he could die soon. This situation presents the need for great courage, perhaps more than the individual has ever known. From where does this courage come? Perhaps the disease itself.

Author and surgeon Bernie S. Siegel knows that "the great lesson people learn from life-threatening illness is the difference between what is and what is not important."[2] Facing mortality can clarify our priorities. When we find out what *is* important, we also find courage.

We need our maps to help us meet novelty as well as catastrophe. It may take a shot of nerve to sing out loud in your car while stuck in traffic. Or to visit the grave of a deceased loved one. Or to show up for your physical exam. Whenever and wherever you find courage, make a mental note. Keep updating your map. Add color and texture without spoiling its simplicity. And never go anywhere without it.

～～  ～～  ～～

I have a friend who has (what she calls) a "courage hat." She wears this peculiar multi-colored, description-defying chapeau whenever she needs "more guts," and she insists that it works. My friend is a nurse who specializes in treating people with AIDS. A spiritual person, she also finds courage through prayer, the support of friends, and through her relationships with her patients. Maybe each source produces a different type of courage. Still, it seems courage can be found in such diverse places as a hat, humanity and the heavens.

To understand what increased courage might do for you, try the following exercise.

Below I am going to give you an incomplete sentence. Finish the sentence as many ways as you can. You might do a better job with it while in a safe, comfortable place. This little procedure may generate some anxiety. In fact, many people have a difficult time developing responses, especially at first. So stick with it for a bit and see what you can learn.

Again, complete the following sentence in as many ways as you can.

*"If I had more courage, I would. . . ."*

*Now, what will you do with what you have learned?*

"Mary Powers, Mary Powers. Show yourself, Mary Powers," chanted the terrified child.

A few seconds pass. Then the visage begins to appear on the mirror in the darkened room. "Ahhhhh!" screams the horrified youngster as he darts for the door.

Sound familiar? "The Evil Mary Powers" lives in most neighborhoods. Although kids call her different names in different regions, the procedure is the same. First comes the seance or the ghost stories to get everyone in the mood. Then, when anxiety soars to a peak, comes the ultimate dare. Who has the guts to call upon the evil Mary Powers? Usually the child with the greatest need to impress (or the one sensible enough to understand how the whole thing works) rises to the occasion. He goes alone into a dark room and stands in front of a mirror for thirty seconds or so. As the seconds tick by (and the eyes adjust to the dark) a face forms in the looking glass. To the child who doesn't understand that he is seeing his own reflection, this turns into an awful experience. What else could it be, he reasons, but the real wicked Mary Powers?

Like other children's games, "The Evil Mary Powers" offers a caricature of the human condition. As we age, we come to realize that few things create more fear, anxiety and angst than an honest look at ourselves. Putting ourselves in situations that reveal our total being may produce what Abraham Maslow described as "a justified fear of being torn apart, of losing control, of being shattered and disintegrated."[3] Overstatement? Well, I'm not sure. Exploration can lead to evidence that contradicts our most comforting beliefs.

I don't doubt that people have reason to approach the unknown cautiously. We could run into monsters, nightmares and things too scary to imagine. Wise folks stroll carefully into uncharted territories. But why venture forth at all? If exploration produces anxiety, why bother? Because if we handle the fear, we may find the treasure. If we face the breakdown, we may achieve a breakthrough. If we stick around long enough to introduce ourselves to wicked Mary Powers, we may master some fear and learn about life.

It has been told that shortly before he died, St. Thomas Aquinas reflected, "If I had my life to live over, I would dare to make more mistakes." St. Thomas knew that hiding from misfortune meant losing part of one's life. In our efforts to protect ourselves from failure we can miss much of what the universe has to offer.

I once heard a sixth grade teacher make a most interesting observation that applies here. A group of educators was discussing how to predict the future performances of children. Most of the people gathered focused on I.Q. and aptitude tests as the method of choice for forecasting academic and vocational abilities. But this particular teacher offered a truly different perspective. She said, "I really don't concern myself with those kinds of test scores when I try to determine how well a child will do. Instead, I look for a particular type of behavior. The child who approaches a project carefully but with determination, this is the kid who will be successful. Most important is how he or she handles failure. The child who reaches an impasse and then stops and thinks and then tries something new, this is the one who will accomplish the most. He or she meets a problem or a mistake, thinks about it, then moves to correct it. It's exciting when you see it. So, no, I don't get too caught up in I.Q. tests. A child's behavior will tell you so much more."

How individuals, be they children or adults, deal with mistakes certainly tells you something about their characters. We all like to think that we will face our defeats and then learn from these experiences. Unfortunately, however, we have a tendency to confuse failure with a terminal illness. Failure can seem irreversible, as if once we enter its grasp we sink into a netherworld of fellow losers. The myth and the reality, though, are worlds apart. As those sixth grade future successes teach us, failure can lead to strength and knowledge.

We don't have to convince ourselves that we enjoy failure (even though mistakes often provide great humor). But in order to live life to the fullest, we probably have to assure ourselves that we can survive — and even laugh about and learn from — setbacks. Even grownups sometimes fall down when they walk. It's a frightening world if you think mishaps can destroy you.

The healthiest among us dare to make mistakes. They acknowledge their miscues, sometimes play with them and, ultimately, learn from them. "The courage to adhere to the truth as we learn it involves the courage to face ourselves with the clear admission of all the mistakes we have made," wrote Buckminster Fuller. "Mistakes are sins only when not admitted." Failure does not have to lead to defeat. Failure leads to shame only if we believe it does.

The fear of messing up may be more common than we

like to believe. In recent years, behavioral scientists have identified a psychological disorder called the "paralyzed perfectionist." The paralyzed perfectionist may appear lazy, apathetic and even bored. On the inside, however, there dwells a great deal of fear. He fears that if he tries anything he could fail and that he could not possibly live with the subsequent shame. So to protect himself from the imagined calamity, he presents an image of indifference. He then rationalizes this by persuading himself, "If I do not try, I cannot fail." And so he lives safe, secure and stagnating.

Not all perfectionists retreat so completely. Many exhaust themselves trying to acquire a flawless appearance. Although their ambitions may be noble, problems arise because they believe they are incapable of living with imperfections even though imperfection is inevitable.

Being human means being less than perfect. Indeed, perfectionism has been referred to as the fear of being human. When you walk through the fear of being human, you learn more and laugh more.

~~ ~~ ~~

Sometimes courage can be frightening. More precisely, because it frequently originates in unusual places, we can be afraid to touch a source of strength. In his book, *Why Am I Afraid To Tell You Who I Am?*, John Powell makes the point that the most often requested song of soldiers, when Bing Crosby visited the South Pacific troops in World War II, was Brahms' "Lullaby." But even if this simple song has proven its power on the battlefield, how many folks would be willing to tap its force today? Aren't we supposed to outgrow this sort of thing?

At Lighthouse, a substance abuse treatment center for adolescents in central Illinois, patients are given teddy bears to accompany them during their stay. Throughout this time these kids need all the security, support and strength they can muster. Although they may resist accepting the bears, often the soft companions become almost permanent attachments to these troubled young people. Many of these kids refer to themselves as "street kids" and they come from worlds with no security blankets or even childhoods. They also abide by a set of street laws — rules that insist that above all else one must appear tough.

There's something striking about the sight of these hardened faces with tattooed arms clutching teddy bears. At first glance, it seems ridiculous . . . then miraculous. The bears soften the faces and encourage the childhood in each child. With this encouragement they are more likely to allow for self-revelation and vulnerability. They become more willing to express needs and ask for help. Accepting the bear is, at first, something of a surrender, a surrender that can lead to recovery.

This story, however, does not end happily ever after. Many of these young souls return to climates that do not sustain teddy bears. Bears can't survive on the streets. Neither can children. Children who live on the streets usually do so without the courage or the ability to get off them. "Tough" then becomes a lifestyle where one is not permitted to look elsewhere for strength.

I could give other examples but I don't think it's necessary. Some people are afraid to pray. Others are too squeamish to talk out loud to themselves in an encouraging way. The point: the road to courage can be frightening.

We might like to think we are above it, but at certain times in our lives we may all need teddy bears and lullabies.

~~ ~~ ~~

One dimension of wisdom must be the ability to tolerate confusion. Without this patience, we would rush to premature conclusions or avoid critical issues altogether.

Life has many mysteries. Those of us fortunate enough to love mysteries soon realize we love life. Confusion can be exciting and/or unsettling; it depends on how you look at it. If you already enjoy delving into the unresolved, this section will have little to offer you. If, however, you shake in the presence of a good dilemma, you need to consider a few things.

Confusion represents another one of those trolls I keep talking about. It makes you stop and consider changing paths. It leaves you unsure and may demand ideas, feelings and behaviors previously foreign to you. Like other obstacles, confusion need not necessarily be destroyed or conquered. Instead it must be respected, perhaps befriended.

Confusion often precedes learning. I once saw a poster on an office door that read: "To wonder is to begin to understand." Confusion provides a certain motivation to explore. Sometimes this exploration leads to answers, other times not. When no resolution appears, confusion presses us to create our own. Thus creativity owes a debt of gratitude to uncertainty. We could also say that to wonder is to begin to create.

Confusion testifies to our freedom. It can teach. It can motivate. It can also humble us. Humility keeps us from thinking we have all the answers. As long as we have humility we will always have things to wonder about. Then we can spend our lives learning and creating.

Mental health professionals have identified hundreds of fears, from arachibutyrophobia (the fear of peanut butter sticking to the roof of one's mouth) to euphobia (the fear of good news) to philosophobia (the fear of philosophy or philosophers). It seems that if you can name it, there is somebody somewhere who's afraid of it.

Not only do people fear negative experiences such as failure, death, car accidents and surgery, but many of us come to dread life's rewards. Long ago psychologists coined the phrase "fear of success" or FOS to describe a fairly common condition that surfaces when the afflicted arrives at the verge of success. At this point, someone with high FOS will sabotage their impending victory.

Sigmund Freud first described the problem in his essay "Those Wrecked by Success." In this paper he described a university professor who worked diligently for thirty years in the hope of succeeding his mentor to a desired chair. Then, upon being offered the position, he became unable to do his work and fell into immobilized confusion. Perhaps a more common example of the fear of success would be the individual who wants to lose a specific amount of weight. He diets successfully until he almost reaches his target then, suddenly, he inexplicably regains all those lost pounds.[4]

People with high FOS frequently excel while contenders but never make it to champions. Something always comes along to rob them of their triumph. While we all have lost a few big games, people with a significant fear of success will make this a fairly consistent pattern. They maintain a high level of performance until they approach what they perceive to be success. Then be it through accident, illness or whatever, the victory eludes them.

A variety of explanations have been presented concerning the fear of success. One view, possibly the most accurate, deserves mention. This particular theory suggests that this fear is rooted in any of a number of irrational beliefs. That is, we all carry with us a collection of beliefs about ourselves and others, as well as about life in general. Ideally, these beliefs are rational and serve to help us become happy, useful and well adjusted. In order to develop and maintain a rational set of beliefs, we must be willing to consider these assumptions from time to time and adjust them when needed. For instance, it is appropriate for a young child to believe she needs an adult to help her cross the street. It would be irrational, however, for most adults to believe this.

Many people who live with a fear of success carry irrational beliefs with them. Early in life — due to discouraging conditions — we may conclude that "I will never amount to anything important," or "Success just never comes to people like me," or "If I become successful at something, people will expect me to always be successful and I'll end up looking like a real failure." Once someone develops a mindset that says, "I can never be successful," they can then repeatedly prove themselves right. This irrational thinking can be difficult to break.

But break it we must. We can, and should, challenge our beliefs. This doesn't necessarily mean change them. Certain beliefs (i.e., the rational ones) must survive. Erroneous notions, however, need erasing. Some of these irrational ideas may have been accurate at an earlier period in our lives. But time can alter reality and failures can become successes. Even folks caught in the "I never win anything" syndrome can have their day.

To people who view themselves as unsuccessful, success represents the uncharted territory discussed earlier. If I've never been there, I might not know how to act when I get there. Do I risk it? Or do I stay with the familiar? The same holds true for happiness. People who have not known happiness can have a difficult time accepting the fact that they *can* find and enter serenity. In other words, people can be afraid of happiness. In order for an unhappy person to become contented, she must ask herself, "Dare I become something I've never been before?"

I suspect that if we could measure the fear in children as they approach Disneyland for the first time, we would find that their anxiety mounts. What appears to be excitement may, in fact, be a fear of experiencing something wonderful yet totally new and unique. By the same token, if we were suddenly given the opportunity to look into heaven, many of us would probably get the jitters while waiting for the pearly gates to open.

On the road to contentment, we walk through fear. Success, in its many forms, represents the conquest of fear.

~~ ~~ ~~

No one avoids fear altogether. Young parents worry about how they will afford their children's college tuition. Then, once the kids have their degrees, mom and dad worry they will marry the wrong people.

During our working years we fret about being audited by the Internal Revenue Service. Then, as we approach retirement, we nervously wonder about the stability of the Social Security system.

A phone that rings in the middle of the night produces anxiety in just about everyone. We tend to fear that the alarm clock won't sound on the morning of the big meeting. No matter how secure we become, we never really lose the anguish that comes with taking off a band-aid. And doesn't it seem that adults are nervous about walking around without shoes?

Fear is as natural as the hiccups. Sometimes — when it comes in small doses — we only need to grin and bear it. It's a lesson older than the Three Stooges. Fear can be funny. If we let it.

"It is not the critic who counts," Gandhi claimed, "nor the man who points out how the strong man stumbles, or where the doer of deeds could have done better. The credit belongs to the man who is actually in the arena; whose face is marred by dust and sweat; who strives valiantly; who errs and may fail again because there is no effort without error or shortcoming, but who does actually strive to do the deeds; who does know the great enthusiasm, the great devotion; who spends himself in a worthy cause; who at the best, knows in the end the triumph of high achievement, and who at the worst, if he fails, at least fails while daring greatly, so that his place shall never be with those cold and timid souls who know neither victory nor defeat."

We can dare to feel "the great enthusiasm" and dare to know "the great devotion." To do so we must touch the force that inspires us to reach as high as the human spirit can soar. We may each touch the force in a different way. It makes itself available to us as we travel our own paths. The force comes to us through our callings.

It's time to move on. We have stopped for a moment to consider fear; now we must refocus our attention on finding courage. Clearly, we will not remove fear from our lives, nor would we want to. Fear serves to protect, educate and motivate us. We would be lost without it.

In Herman Melville's novel *Moby Dick*, Starbuck — the chief mate of the whaling ship, Pequod — warns, "I will have no man on my boat who is not afraid of a whale."

"By this, he seemed to mean," interprets Melville, "not only that a most reliable and useful courage was that which arises from the fair estimation of the encountered peril, but that an utterly fearless man is a far more dangerous comrade than a coward."

Yes, it's time to move on. We need to resume our search for courage. We should not be surprised or discouraged when fear again arises. We have found it to be a friend, a teacher, an opponent, a clown or an illusion. We deal with fear as it presents itself — by respecting it, learning from it, conquering it, laughing with it, or seeing through it.

Above all, we must never let fear keep us from finding the great enthusiasm for life.

*Where there is no vision, the people perish.*
Ecclesiastes

*We need at least three things in order to live
happy and meaningful lives — something to do,
someone to love, and something to hope for.*
Unknown

CHAPTER  IV

# *Daring To Dream*

We all need dreams. Some people don't know this. Some
people have no dreams. But we all need dreams.

Think about it. What do you hope to accomplish in the
next year? What would you like to do with the rest of your
life? If you could change one thing about this world of ours,
what would it be? And (if you're not), why aren't you trying
to improve it?

I'm sorry . . . I'm preaching. When one begins talking
about dreams, it's tempting to start pontificating. It's a message that fits well into the fire and brimstone (even "holier
than thou") presentations. I shall try to avoid this. It has
been done to death anyway. Let's see if we can take a walk
into the world of dreams and visions and see what we can
see.

"In the story of the Ugly Duckling, when did the Ugly Duckling stop feeling Ugly?" asks Benjamin Hoff in *The Tao of Pooh*. "When he realized that he was a Swan. Each of us has something Special, a Swan of some sort, hidden inside somewhere. But until we recognize that it's there, what can we do but splash around treading water? The Wise are Who They Are. They work with what they've got and do what they can do. . . . For within the Ugly Duckling is the Swan, inside the Bouncy Tiger is the Rescuer who knows the Way, and in each of us is something Special, and that we need to keep."[1]

We hold on to our something Special by allowing it to emerge and then keeping it alive. We allow it to appear by accepting the simple notion that each of us can be more than we are today. This is not to say that what we are today is inadequate. Rather, we can be more than we are today. Confusing? Well, let's stay with it.

Once that something Special presents itself we keep it alive by keeping it in sight. Perhaps the most confusing thing about being human is that we can turn away from what we really are. Our real self never goes away, but we can distract ourselves and then call these distractions reality. We need to focus our attention on matters that move us.

Dreamers have two special qualities. First, they welcome inspiration. Second, they stay in touch with their sources of inspiration, rarely turning away to search for safer yet less fulfilling alternatives. With every act of courage you tell the world, "This is me!" With every dream you recognize you tell *yourself*, "This is me!"

It takes courage to dream. To fulfill a vision can mean a lot of work; it can also mean risking quite a bit. A prominent middle-aged attorney may be frightened by a recurring desire to leave his practice to become a farmer. A college senior, facing strong family pressure to enter medical school, may recognize a growing urge to enter the field of social work. Both of these cases point to the fact that living a dream may involve moving away from security and support.

Our dreams also include so much more than careers. Ask yourself these questions. What kind of person do I want to be? Do I want to be honest, assertive, generous, curious, kind, compassionate? What qualities do I need to be true to who I really am? And if I decide to try to develop one personal quality in the next year, what will it be?

I know a college chaplain who has an interesting approach to help students find their dreams. During the course of his workshops, he has the participants write their own eulogies as a way of giving them the opportunity to describe how they would like to be remembered after their lives end. In spite of the initial anxiety, this exercise comes to teach several powerful lessons. Perhaps most important of all is the discovery that they want to be remembered as having contributed something. As they write through their fears, they come to understand what they need to contribute. In so doing they find dreams. Then they face the question of what they will do with what they have learned.

But we are getting ahead of ourselves. In the next chapter we will deal with how one acts on a vision. Our present challenge is to dare to dream — big dreams and little dreams. Listen for them, fight for them, nurture and protect them. We all deserve time to dream.

The dreams we must hold on to are those we cannot let go of. They make themselves known in many ways. Like lighthouses, once lit, they beckon us to move in a special direction.

For a time, dreams may remain below the surface, waiting for the right conditions before making their presence known. They do not stay forever hidden. "The unrealized self demands visibility," insists Leo Buscaglia. "It cannot be ignored for long. . . . We are aware that there is something missing and we have a desperate need to discover what it is."[2]

Sometimes we may have difficulty finding a single vision to call our own. A psychologist friend of mine described this state as "waiting to see the next step." On other occasions we seem to be flooded by images of what our lives could or should be. In these cases we have to make some hard decisions. We have to invest ourselves in the visions that seem vital. Certain dreams have more power than others. They give us the feeling that somehow they pertain specifically to us. For example, we would all like to win the lottery, even people who never play the lottery. There is nothing about this fantasy that points to anyone in particular and, other than luring one to buy a ticket, it does not provide much direction.

On the other hand, there are people like David, a bright, energetic, thirty-three-year-old pathologist. Already quite successful in his career, he could not escape the feeling that his talent and education needed to be applied elsewhere. After some consideration, he cut back his practice to three days a week and began writing short stories. He admits he does not need to be a best-selling author or a Pulitzer Prize winner. He does, however, find fulfillment in his writing. As he described to me these adjustments in his life, I found myself feeling glad for him, glad that he had the chutzpa to reach for something out of the ordinary, yet tremendously important to him. I also had the sense that his fiction would lead him to his next step, that it wasn't so much a destination as a path.

Dreams loom larger than life but they should not be confused with fantasy. We sit back and watch fantasy. Dreams, however, take us out of the role of spectator and move us to the brink of action. Visions do not owe their existences to fantasy; rather, they are sustained by hope.

"In the middle of winter I learned at last that I carried within myself an invincible summer," penned Albert Camus. In the midst of our darkest hours we carry with us the potential for hope. The idea that one can be "hopeless" is as erroneous as the notion that one can be "thoughtless." Humans are never without thought just as we are never without hope. But sometimes we lose sight of the hope that always lives within. Hope is as natural as laughter; we never lose the ability to hope or to laugh, even when we have not hoped or laughed for a long time.

"There is a hope that acts as an explosive, and a hope that disciplines and infuses patience. The difference is between the immediate hope and the distant hope," suggests philosopher Eric Hoffer. Hope can lead to miracles. Or it can lead to the understanding that some good things take time.

Certain visions belong to today, others to tomorrow. We build big dreams with smaller ones. The dreams we must hold on to are the ones we just cannot let go of. Fortunately these relentless dreams — if we pay attention to them — carry with them the hope and the energy needed to get us started.

A dream can be difficult to maintain. A mirage calls us onward even when we feel frustrated and exhausted. It's

often easier and safer to stay put and escape the risks necessary to realize a vision. And once we admit a dream, either to
ourselves or to others, we feel a push to reach for that goal, a
push that may require us to make changes and become more
visible in our striving. By acknowledging a goal, we set up
the possibility of falling short of that objective, a possibility
that can stir much anxiety.

Abraham Maslow called this phenomenon "The Jonah
Complex," and described it as "the fear of one's own greatness" or "the evasion of one's destiny" or the "running away
from one's own best talents." This concerned Professor
Maslow who saw our culture losing the creations and accom-
plishments of some of our greatest hearts and minds solely
because they are afraid to dream the vital dreams.

> I have found it easy enough to demonstrate this to my
> students simply by asking, "Which of you in the class hopes
> to write the great American novel, or to be a Senator, or
> Governor or President? Who wants to be Secretary Gen-
> eral of the United Nations? Or a great composer? Who
> among you will be a great leader?" Generally, everybody
> starts giggling, and squirming until I ask, "If not you, then
> who else?". . . (Then) I'll say, "What great book are you
> now secretly planning to write?" And then they often
> blush and stammer and push me off in some way. But why
> should I not ask the question? Who else will write the
> books on psychology except psychologists? So I can ask,
> "Do you not plan to be a psychologist?" "Well, yes." "Are
> you in training to be a mute or inactive psychologist?
> What's the advantage of that? That's not a good path to
> self-actualization. No, you must want to be a first class
> psychologist, meaning the very best you are capable of
> becoming. If you deliberately plan to be less than you are
> capable of being, then I warn you that you will be deeply
> unhappy for the rest of your life. You will be evading your
> own capacities, your own possibilities."[3]

I've never met a person who couldn't improve the world. I have, however, met folks who — in spite of this potential — were afraid to make their contributions to the planet. Maybe the biggest difference between those who do and those who don't is that those who do are the ones who believe they can.

Gandhi was right. Those who try never really fail. If we accept the call of our visions, we will never be defeated.

An old Mexican tale tells of the day the devil decided to go out of business. He sent word throughout the land that he would be auctioning off all the devices he used to tempt people and lead them astray. And, as he expected, people came from near and far prepared to pay great sums of money for the devil's instruments.

Politicians, businessmen, salesmen, and many others who believed they could benefit from owning the devil's tools all came to the auction. Lonely people, frightened people, as well as all those other souls looking for short-cuts to strength and happiness flocked to the event.

When the moment arrived for the sale to begin, the room buzzed with excitement. Participants fidgeted with delight waiting for the opportunity to purchase the power of Satan. Then the auction began.

One by one the items were placed on the block. To everyone's surprise, however, all the objects looked shiny and new as if they had never been used. As a result, the bidding moved along slowly as buyers waited for an implement that had already proven its effectiveness.

Finally, that moment came. One of the devil's helpers brought to the stage an old worn device. Immediately everyone took notice of the unusual article. Although no one recognized it, they all felt certain that this must be something quite powerful.

While the crowd buzzed, a potential buyer asked one of Satan's aides what this strange object was.

"Oh, that," replied the devil's assistant, "is Satan's favorite and most frequently utilized tool. It's what you humans call despair. You see, Satan has found that once he can get someone to give up hope, he can do with them pretty much what he pleases."

At times it's best to deal with the cold hard facts. At other times, it's not. The facts loom before the naked eye, but our sight is imperfect. Life contains more than we can see, touch, taste, smell, and hear. If we accept this, we may become sensitive to new and vitalizing qualities of life. The dreams we build our futures on may only loosely reflect reality. Yet these imaginative expectations have their place. Like the exhausted traveler who delays his collapse in order to reach the mirage, we sense things in the distance that seem to pull us further along our journey in life. Sometimes these mirages disappear as we reach them, but by then we are often in sight of genuine shelter. Illusions motivate.

In recent years psychologists have performed a number of experiments to determine if depressed people have a distorted view of reality. Prior to the start of this research, few would have predicted the results. The researchers have found that not only do mild to moderately depressed people have a clear outlook on reality, they judge reality *better* than non-depressed individuals.[4] One particular group of researchers at Stanford University, for example, found that depressed people are often more realistic in their self-perceptions than are non-depressed people. While the depressed subjects saw their abilities more accurately, as measured by an objective evaluation, the others saw their own abilities as more positive than they really were. The researchers suggest that an "illusory glow" of competence might be good for mental health.[5] This indicates that healthy people have a certain healthy insanity. They see more than *what is*. They also see what *could be*.

What one person calls denial, another might call hope. A "never say die" attitude in the face of adversity does not necessarily suggest that one misunderstands the *facts*. Rather, people who keep hope alive seem to comprehend more than the facts; they allow for the possibility that the future cannot be foretold by the immediate present.

Hope can heal. Indeed there are times when only hope can clear the road to recovery. Veterans of Alcoholics Anonymous, for instance, routinely encourage those new to sobriety by simply saying, "It gets better." To someone struggling through the withdrawal, confusion and a multitude of mixed-up feelings, this reminder puts a light at the end of the tunnel. Coming from someone who really knows, it can be a powerful directive. It provides hope.

The same lesson applies to those facing grief. In studies designed to discern what helps people get through bereavement, a striking finding emerges. Grieving people benefit significantly by hearing from others who have survived similar losses. Hearing that even though things may never be the same, they will get better, helps supply hope to what can feel like a hopeless situation.

Anyone can tell a suffering soul, "It gets better." But there are those who — because they have traveled a like passageway — possess a special ability to bestow hope. This gift that rises from tragedy can be seen in the growing number of support groups developing around the world. In these organizations, more healed survivors help less healed survivors largely through the transmission of hope. These groups help people through divorce, the aftermath of child abuse, cancer, mental illness and many other kinds of misfortune.

Like courage itself, we each strengthen our hope in special ways. A certain person, place, or passage can ignite faith, inspire optimism, and make the future a friend again. And hope can build when we are reminded of things we have known all along. Things like the words of Max Ehrmann.

> Be at peace with God, whatever you conceive Him to be. And whatever your labors and aspirations, in the noisy confusion of life, keep peace in your soul. With all its sham, drudgery and broken dreams, it is still a beautiful world.

We can't put everything into words. Certain qualities and experiences produce more power than can be contained in mere terms. At times we can only approximate through words the immensity of a particular trait. W.W. Woodbridge knew this well long ago when he wrote his little book, *That Something*:

> Until we wake "that something" of the soul, we live as a horse lives. We bear on our muscle those that have found "that something" and we bear them up on the mountain, to take their places among the masters of men; "that something" lies dormant in every soul until aroused; with many, it sleeps until the last great sleep. Sometimes it does not wake until man stands tottering on the border of the grave;

sometimes it is found by the child, playing by its mother's knee. . . . A man's success depends alone on "that something." "That something" of his soul. Abraham Lincoln found it when a lad. It warmed the cold floor on which he lay and studied. It added light to the flickering glow of the wood fire, that he might see to read. "That something" is an awful force. It made Edison the great man of his age. It made Carnegie, Woodrow Wilson, Roosevelt.[6]

We can identify many others including the likes of Joan of Arc, Dorothea Dix, Helen Keller and Mother Teresa who have also touched "that something" in their souls. Moreover, we could all compose a list of folks who have never caught history's spotlight but who have taken "that something" and used it to make lasting improvements in their causes and communities.

Unfortunately, as Woodbridge points out, in some people "that something" sleeps until their deaths. But we must bear in mind that this force exists always and in everyone. We can try to ignore it but we cannot destroy it. If we have chloroformed "that something" within us it may be difficult to revitalize. More often though, when we come to give it our consideration we realize that it has been screaming for attention all along . . . screams that may have produced restlessness and boredom. It takes a certain chutzpa to greet the unknown. Even the unknown within us.

We all have dreams. Sadly, some folks never find them.

Again, it's time to move on . . . time to consider how visions turn into action. A most important step this; we should tread carefully.

Someone once remarked that in life you have to compromise ninety-eight percent of the time but don't you dare compromise on that last two percent! This two percent represents our convictions, our most fundamental and sacred hopes and beliefs. And then there was the Japanese martial arts instructor I had in college who, while we trained, would scream, "You must be prepared to die!" He tried to teach us *"bushido"* — the way of the warrior. It seemed so ridiculous to think of college karate as worth dying for. But absurdity, of course, has its lessons. Perhaps we were too young to understand, or maybe Americans have difficulty comprehending that we can prepare for those times when we have to put it all on the line to live out our convictions.

Fulfilling a dream often requires a struggle of some kind. Yet if it is one of those visions you cannot let go of, the struggle must occur. To do otherwise would mean abandoning that special calling meant specifically for you. During the course of a lifetime, you may have hundreds of visions that come and go. A select few call to be acted upon.

We have considered the dream before beginning the act because the dream deserves time to itself. Once a vision starts to emerge it must be nurtured and protected. We can play with it and think it through for a while. If we care for it properly and it strengthens and withstands the test of time, then we are called to act.

Some dreams, in their early stages of development, are too weak to encourage our efforts to achieve them. The child who dreams of being a physician is not ready for medical school. But if the vision continues to grow, it may sustain her through all the obstacles she will face on the way to her goal. In other words, give a dream time to be a dream. Attend to it. See what it does. Only then will you be able to distinguish a calling from a passing fancy.

If you pay attention to your visions, you will know when it is time to act on them. Once a dream becomes strong, it produces courage. Like the athlete who uses mental imagery to see himself successfully complete his purpose even before he begins, in our minds we see ourselves fulfilling missions that seem right to us. We then feel pulled toward these visions. A dream that has been nurtured and protected provides us with the courage needed to begin reaching for its fulfillment.

*If we don't leave the world a better place
than how we found it, then what's the point?*
Father McCabe
from the television series St. Elsewhere

*Whatever you can do,
or dream you can, begin it.
Boldness has genius, power and magic in it.*
Johann Wolfgang von Goethe

CHAPTER V

# *Choosing To Act*

The leap from inclination to action can be a large one. The daring soul who always wanted to skydive finds his moment of truth while staring face to face with a cloud. The dream may have gotten him this far but now he must decide whether or not to make the dream come true. Between a dream and an act lies a choice.

The fellow who jumps and the one who stays on the plane may have had a lot in common up until they made their decisions. But they took different paths after that point and, consequently, became very different people. One realized a dream and thus became stronger and more alive.

He encountered the thrill of flying through fear. The other gentleman either cowered from the opportunity to fulfill a vision or, perhaps, learned — while at his moment of truth — that this act was not worth the risk, that this dream was not as important as he had thought. We are not in a position to judge. What looks like cowardice may be reason (and, of course, vice versa). Discretion may indeed be the better part of valor.

I used to wish I could travel in a submarine. I thought it would be exhilarating to journey beneath the sea in that silent fascinating world. This childhood fantasy lasted for years . . . up until I had the chance to enter the dream. While visiting the Philadelphia Navy Yard, I toured a partially submerged submarine. To my astonishment, I hated the experience almost as soon as it began. I felt like I was stuck in a tube of toothpaste. It just wasn't the way I pictured it. Did I "chicken out" or did I learn something? Well, I don't know. But I'm glad I went down into that sub. I came out with room for a new dream. Maybe this is what growing up is all about.

There comes a time when you must act on your dreams. Sometimes you can plan for this act, other times not. If you want to be an honest person, your honesty will be tested again and again, suddenly and unexpectedly. So too if you hope to be a generous or a kind soul. Life will ask you to act like the person you desire to be.

We live in a time when "self-improvement" has become big business. We find ourselves surrounded by experts advising us on everything from how to lose weight to how to gain confidence. We are led to believe that if we abide by their advice we can be more productive, more assertive and more relaxed. And if your first set of gurus can't remove all your faults, another group will offer their views on how to live with your indelible flaws. At no time in history has there been more advice given. Consequently, we have more confusion than at any other point in time. We live in the age of advice and confusion.

An individual who wants to improve herself need go no further than the local bookstore (or so it seems). There she can study under the masters of happiness, slimness and other noble intentions. Although these authorities frequently disagree with each other, they can be quite effective in persuading audiences that their message is *the* answer.

As a result, we see a new breed of consumers who buy the "self-improvement" books and read them through and through, find every available audio and video tape and listen carefully to each word and then, if they can find no new material, go back and read and listen to the same old information again. They hope. They dream. But until they begin to act there is little improvement. Unfortunately, many self-improvement addicts spend all their days in the planning stage.

To fulfill a dream, we must be prepared to fail. Then, should failure occur, we are better prepared to pick ourselves up and reconsider the dream. If the dream remains, we must refocus on how to approach the act.

"Activity must not be confused with courage, although there is no courage without activity," suggested Alfred Adler.[1] When afraid, we may try to engage in safe yet useless activity such as pacing, fidgeting or nail biting, but these are hardly courageous. Courage involves acting on what you believe to be right, not just acting aimlessly. It takes gumption to dream. It takes even more fortitude to test the dream by moving to realize it.

Moving to realize a dream can mean moving into uncertainty, uncertainty that can lead to rejection, humiliation, failure or other sour experiences. Still, we feel called to fulfill our dreams. "We have to face the fact that we must constantly make decisions on the basis of incomplete evidence," insists philosopher Joseph Fabry. "Columbus never would have discovered America had he waited for all the information on which to base his decision to start out on his journey. . . . Our life is not regulated at every crossing by a red light that tells us to stop or a green light that tells us to go ahead. We live in an era of flashing yellow lights that leave the decision to the individual."[2]

In this era of flashing yellow lights we encounter a plethora of advisors who point us in every direction. We know we have to move somewhere in order to find or create a purpose in our lives. Ultimately, however, if and how we move is up to each of us.

When Khrushchev made his famous denunciation of Stalin, a solitary voice in the Congress Hall was heard to say, "Where were you, Comrade Khrushchev, when all these innocent people were being slaughtered?"

Khrushchev paused a moment, looked around the hall and said, "Will the man who said that kindly stand up?"

Tension mounted in the hall. No one spoke. No one moved.

Then Khrushchev said, "Well, whoever you are, you have your answer now. I was in exactly the same position then as you are now."[3]

It seems we have run into a paradox. That's right, a paradox. You know, a contradiction of sorts that somehow makes sense. Acts of courage are paradoxical in that we must be committed to the act, but we must also be aware at the same time that we might possibly be wrong.[4] In other words, real courage has a humble nature. Whereas fearlessness is often rooted in ignorance, courage acknowledges danger and uncertainty. We can move in the face of uncertainty. What we believe is right is not always the same as what we know for sure. This world provides precious little certainty. In order to find total surety, we would first have to achieve narrow-mindedness. So we're probably better off to accept some confusion and then look for the courage to act in spite of the bewilderment.

Perhaps one of the most confusing paths is the road to becoming a good person. We don't have to own the road to travel it. We simply have to follow where we believe it leads. And eventually, if we stay on this path, we find that the destination has become a part of us.

Shortly after I had moved to St. Louis, I came across a very troubled bear. He lived in the bear section of the zoo right next to the entrance.

St. Louisans are justifiably proud of the zoo. To those who have never seen it I can only describe it as beautiful. The accommodations for the animals seem better than home as they each have plenty of room to roam, good food and no predators. To human visitors, it looks like a splendid place for an animal to settle down and raise a family. But even in the best places problems can arise.

On this particular day I came across a most unusual event. I entered this magnificent zoo and the first creature I saw was a bear whom I will call Maurice. I found Maurice in the midst of a completely natural setting consisting of rocks, foliage and a rather large pond. Maurice's home appeared natural . . . but Maurice did not. He didn't stroll around his small forest like the other beasts. Instead, he paced back and forth, back and forth. Six and a half steps forward, a sudden turn and then six and a half steps back, on and on. He must have been doing this for quite a while because the other bears looked bored by it. They weren't giving him a second thought.

I, however, was fascinated. Why would Maurice pace so? And why wouldn't he take advantage of all the space provided? Prior to this, the only zoos I had ever known housed their animals in small cages. For that reason, I never really liked zoos. I saw nothing appealing about animals confined to cages so I stayed away from them for quite some time. Then, upon my return, the first creature I encountered acted as if he didn't want the freedom after all.

Certain mysteries never get resolved and such was the case with Maurice, for a time anyway. No one I knew could explain the pacing bear. I didn't give up easily but, as the years passed without a clue, I came to accept that either Maurice was simply crazy or this was just another example of God's sense of humor.

Long after I had stopped pursuing an answer — and over five years after I had first met Maurice — the light came on. Miraculously, and quite unintentionally, I came across an article on animal behavior that explained Maurice. While reading the paper I also came to understand why it had been so important for me to understand this peculiar bear.

Maurice, it seems, was making a point about courage. When certain animals are raised in cages, they have a tendency to view their world as being the size of their quarters. If they remain caged long enough, the cage becomes a part of their psyches. Then, should they be released, the pattern continues. Hence Maurice's repetitious pacing. He lacked the courage to move any further.

I don't know what happened to Maurice. The next time I visited the zoo — about a year after I had first met him — he was gone. Maybe he ended up too stressed out and needed to be returned to a safe little cage. Perhaps the zoo decided he wasn't their kind of bear. In a setting that cost millions of dollars to appear natural, Maurice's behavior looked mechanical. Another alternative could be that he died. Maybe he felt inescapably trapped in his mental cage and lost the will to live.

I think I was supposed to meet Maurice. Carl Jung once postulated that if you trace coincidence back far enough, you will find it was inevitable. Meeting Maurice and then stumbling on to the explanation of his behavior struck me, in hindsight, as somehow inevitable. I don't know if this lesson was necessarily preordained but I always suspected that it was supposed to happen. If a psychology professor had taught me about mental cages, I doubt if the point would have taken root as deep as it did. The message needed a demonstration. And the fact that it found expression in such a simple way added to its power.

The lesson becomes even more powerful when we consider that at some time or another, there may be a little Maurice in all of us.

At those points when we need to act in the face of fear, we can benefit from a little extra push. We don't always need a tornado-like force to move us, but rather a nudge to get us rolling. This gentle shove can begin with a special set of words. Words that carry strength.

We all need our own favorite inspirational passages.

Statements that aim to inspire exist in ample supply. But finding the right one — the one that really encourages us to be true to ourselves — can take some doing. Words have power, a power we can overlook. Finding a favorite quote or a list of favorite sayings, however, is a time-proven means of finding courage. For centuries people have looked to particular passages from the Bible or other venerable sources to provide the strength to do what they believe is right.

There are plenty of inspiring lines. We need to find the ones that speak directly to us. And if you cannot find them, maybe that means you need to write your own. As George Bernard Shaw once observed, "The people who get on in this world are the people who get up and look for the circumstances they want and, if they can't find them, make them."

For years I kept in my wallet a little passage I had clipped from a magazine that read: "People don't fail, they only stop trying." Fortunately, by the time the wallet was stolen, I had committed these words of wisdom to memory. I just hope whoever took the wallet noticed the words and understood their value. Maybe that scrap of paper found its way to the person who needed it most.

Football coaches scream, "No guts, no glory!" and "When the going gets tough, the tough get going!" Catchy phrases can certainly energize. But to maximize the power of a passage, we need to look for one that has a special meaning to us. Maybe it's something your grandmother used to say or a line from a poem that no one else seems to notice. It's the statement, or statements, that seem addressed especially to you.

Find the words that give you courage. Keep them with you. Put them in your memory and, when necessary, put them in front of your eyes. Hang them on your walls or put them in a locket on a chain around your neck. Repeat these words often but never take them for granted. Make them a friend and you won't be intimidated by their power. More than anything, stay close to words that move you.

~~ ~~ ~~

"You're only young once." Or so they say. And everything we do motivated by this slogan seems to make us age. But that's O.K. After all, we're only young once. The happiest among us, though, seem to be young once and for always.

One of the best ways to stay young is to try new experiences. See new places, meet new people, read new books, ask new questions. True, new experiences have a way of causing anxiety but they also tend to bring happiness. Among our lists of funny memories, we have a knack for recalling all those awkward "first times" such as the first date, the first drivers' license test, the birth of one's first child, buying that first car, the first house, and the first time you became convinced that the world was coming to an end. We can stay young at heart as long as we provide ourselves with significant first time experiences. It's another one of those peculiar paradoxes: the courage needed to grow older is much the same as the courage required to remain young.

Folks can be frightened by challenges that are not "supposed" to be met by people in their age group. Intelligent, curious, middle-aged individuals, for example, often deny their dream of finishing college because they feel too old to start. For instance, a forty-five-year-old man who has always wanted to attend college might say, "Since I can only go part-time, it could take me eight years to get my degree!" If you ever meet this man, ask him how old he will be in eight years. Then, ask him how old he will be in eight years if he receives a college degree along the way. The only difference is that if he does not attend college he will still be eight years older but without having fulfilled his dream.

Saying, "I'm too old" — though at times accurate — can be a socially acceptable form of cowardice. No one ever became too old to find courage. So no one need retreat from excitement and exploration.

Since we live in the age of insurance, we can add to our policies whenever life gets a little frightening. Insurance represents a popular modern day form of security. This is why the salespeople come out of the woodwork when we come to the verge of a major life change. College seniors approaching graduation and "the real world" meet, usually for the first time, the life insurance vendor offering an unexpected form of protection. Then, as the wedding nears, more salespeople try to tempt you to insure everything from your life to your lunch money. And so it goes in the days before the arrival of your first-born. I'm not sure how it works when one approaches retirement, but I won't be surprised to find myself, once again, surrounded by the insurance people. I can only conclude that this must be a fact of human existence. Whenever we come to a crossroads in life, we can be sure to find at least three things — opportunity, some anxiety and someone trying to sell insurance.

Wouldn't it be wonderful if, at these pivotal points, we could also find someone or something willing and able to give us courage? Hopefully, by now it has become clear that the question is not, "Is that someone or something really there?" Rather, the correct question is, "Can we find it?"

I wonder how many hours the average person spends worrying during the course of a lifetime. If such a statistic could be accurately measured, the figure might be staggering. In fact, it might even prove that worrying is one of our most popular activities. Maybe things were different back in "simpler times" but we have evolved into a tribe of worriers.

Behaviorists tell us that people will maintain a particular behavior if adequately reinforced for doing so. At first glance we can miss the rewards fretting brings. Only after a little thought does it become apparent that many worriers see benefits in this activity. You have to understand that the vast majority of the things we worry about never happen. So inside themselves, many worriers believe that if they worry about a catastrophe, the misfortune will be prevented. Let me give an example.

When I was in third grade a religion teacher with a flair for the dramatic described for the class the events that will occur when the world "comes to an end." She told us it would happen suddenly, by fire, *when no one was thinking about it* (italics mine). Now the part about the fire set even the most angelic kids fidgeting. But it was her afterthought (i.e., "when no one is thinking about it") that hooked me. For the longest time after that I thought constantly about the end of the world, reasoning that if I kept it in mind it wouldn't happen. I figured I was doing humanity quite a favor. (And no, no one ever thanked me. You see, fortunately, I kept my delusion to myself. I did, however, learn about worrying.)

If we could remember all the things we've worried about in our lives we would have a lot to laugh about. The new house didn't collapse the day after you bought it nor did the new car get stolen. The baby was born without a mermaid's tail and then began to walk and talk right on schedule. People didn't notice your perspiration or the fact that you couldn't remember if it's "who" or "whom." In all likelihood your friends don't know that embarrassing secret you're keeping and, what's more, they probably wouldn't like you any less even if they did. The dentures fit perfectly and were not nearly the trouble you feared they might be. And through it all, you've managed to keep your dignity and sense of humor.

We may not be able to avoid all worry. But the trick to surviving it is to do something about it. If you're worried about a lump on your arm, go to the doctor. If your job is killing you, start looking for a new one. Worry feeds on excuses. If at all possible, do something about the cause of your fears. When you walk through a fear, you walk to courage. We build courage by facing, and dealing with, fear. There certainly is power in positive thinking. But the power comes through the doing.

There are, however, times when it seems no action exists that can correct a situation. Parents, for example, waiting outside an operating room while their child undergoes surgery can feel helpless. They can't assist in the operation. They can't go back in time and prevent the malady. They feel paralyzed.

When people feel desperate, they frequently end up praying. Maybe there are no atheists in hospital waiting rooms either. In any case, I've noticed that spiritual people are never helpless. They always have something powerful to *do*.

Sometimes spiritual folks pray for miracles, especially when miracles appear to be their only hope. But at other times, it seems that praying for miracles is not as helpful as praying for courage.

Life can hurt. No one has found a way to change this. Courage, no matter how strong, cannot make our lives pain-free.

Certain hurts, the small ones, last only a short time. The swelling goes down, the frustration turns to humor, the day ends and a new one begins. The pain fades, just as we knew it would.

Then there are the events so devastating that the possibility of recovery looks, at best, uncertain. A friend struggling through a difficult divorce described it this way, "You wake up in the morning, sit up in bed. You feel the floor underneath your feet. And then it hits you. . . . Oh, God! It wasn't a dream."

Nightmares surrender to alarm clocks. Real tragedy takes it own time. It lingers and builds waves of emotion that crash into feeble plans to "get on with" one's life. Every time one tries to get up, along comes that force to test one's stability.

Perhaps the most common form of serious tragedy comes through the loss of a loved one. The grieving soul tends to wonder if things will ever get better. Some experts say that after a major loss you have to go through the seasons (i.e., at least one year) before life returns to normal. Other authorities insist that three years is a more accurate estimate. Still others suggest that grieving is such an individual experience that we can learn little by discussing "norms."

Recovering from loss means facing a great deal of sorrow, anger and uncertainty. Bereavement represents one of life's most difficult monsters. We face most of our other dragons knowing we have the support of the people closest to us. Not so with grief. After the death of a loved one, we meet the devastating aftermath without the support of that special person.

The devastation is no mystery. Even those who have never experienced such a loss can imagine the torment. What remains an enigma is how people survive such experiences and then, eventually, return to a caring and productive lifestyle. Although grieving people rarely feel courageous, they offer true examples of courage.

And then there are those extraordinary individuals who find something special in these darkest hours. Something that transforms their existences by providing a mission. For instance, nothing could have prepared Norma Phillips for the sudden death of her daughter, Sherry, who was killed by a drunk driver at the age of sixteen. The event, however, gave her life a valuable new direction as she founded the organization *Mothers Against Drunk Driving* (MADD), which seeks to impose stiffer penalties on those convicted of driving under the influence of alcohol. Similarly, John Walsh, whose six-year-old son Adam was kidnapped and murdered, turned this senseless slaughter into a national network of child-finding services that identifies missing children and develops ways to locate them.[5] Losses that may have destroyed many, led Norma Phillips and John Walsh into new dimensions that have saved, and will continue to save, others from the anguish they have known.

Poet Sam Keen once reflected, "I have learned one important thing in my life — how to begin again." Each time we begin again we are different than we were at our last start. Every event and circumstance can teach us. The worst devastation can lead to miraculous results. Life can hurt. No one has found a way to change this. Somehow, some people find something in tragedy that points them toward their mission. Exactly how this mission is arranged, I can only wonder.

But I do know that there is nothing more marvelous than one who has known real tragedy and yet looks hopefully and lovingly upon the world. We have no right to expect this from anyone. It defies what appears to be logic. Still, courageous souls have taught us that devastation can lead to determination. Mourning can lead to a sense of mission. In short, sometimes people find courage and a sense of purpose while in a most ravaged state.

~ ~ ~

A widow in her late sixties, who had lived in the same apartment for twenty-five years, came home one day to find that her apartment had been robbed. Confused and afraid, she decided to move. When the moving company arrived she became even more frightened. She felt they were stealing her belongings and drawing strange cult symbols on her furniture. When her possessions arrived at her new residence, she left many of them in boxes.

The world continued to become more terrifying for her. She believed the people in her new neighborhood were following her and secretly signaling to each other. Finally, she was referred to a psychiatrist who prescribed tranquilizers, but her experiences did not change. A second psychiatrist diagnosed her as having a paranoid thought disorder and recommended hospitalization. She refused, however, because she thought this doctor might be trying to hurt her.

A third psychiatrist took an entirely different approach. He explained to the woman that she had "lost her shell" — her previous apartment, her old neighborhood and the people in that neighborhood. At this point, like any other crustacean that has lost its shell, she was vulnerable. In such a fragile state, she grew suspicious of just about everything. Until she found adequate protection, her condition would likely deteriorate.

The psychiatrist advised her to unpack all her belongings, hang up the pictures and other articles that decorated her previous apartment, put the books on the shelves and organize the apartment so that it became familiar. She was not to make new friends in her new neighborhood for two weeks but, in the meantime, she was to reestablish contact with her old friends. In brief, she was to build a healthy new shell.

The woman followed the doctor's advice and her symptoms disappeared rapidly.[6]

When we stray from our avenues to courage, we become vulnerable. To those in this unprotected state, the world becomes a dangerous place, a place where we can easily become hurt and humiliated. We all need a home, a safe place, where we can retreat to build more strength. There are two kinds of safe places. One offers only a place to hide. The other — the healthy shell — provides access to courage. Here we find what we need to walk bravely into what can be a scary world.

So if you don't already have one, ask yourself, "If I were going to arrange a safe place for myself that contained as many roads to courage as I could find, what would it look like? What would it feel like?"

Few things bolster self-esteem more than the knowledge that one can act courageously when confronted by fear. We need confidence, not that we can remove fear, but that we can tap the courage that fills the universe.

Thus far we have found a number of avenues to courage. These routes are, however, unlimited. Just as we all have our own paths to travel in life, we each have our own tracks to strength. Folks find courage through laughter, a good cry, a special book, friendships, a hat and inspirational passages. Fortitude can also come to us by way of prayer, a family portrait, tragedy, a special symbol, a good night's sleep, memories and visions. The list could go on and on. No matter how long we run the list, though, it will always be a simple list. All roads to courage are simple roads.

Once we develop the faith that courage exists and that it can be counted on, we encounter life more honestly and with fewer distortions and defenses. We are then more likely to hear all the messages, not just the ones that keep us safe and unchallenged. Then and only then can we hear that special calling directed to each one of us. And then and only then will we be brave enough to act on what we hear.

*I don't know what your destiny will be,*
*but one thing I know: the only ones among you*
*who will be really happy are those who*
*will have sought and found how to serve.*

Albert Schweitzer

*My mission on earth is to recognize the void*
*— inside and outside of me — and fill it.*

Rabbi Menahem-Mendl

*The only true joy in life is being used for a*
*purpose recognized by yourself as a mighty one.*

Bertrand Russell

CHAPTER VI

# *Pursuing Your Special Calling*

My five-year-old daughter Colleen hid one of my slippers
the other day. Although still in an early morning haze, I
stumbled around in an unproductive effort to find it. When
it dawned on me (by way of her giggling) that she was behind
the prank, I insisted that she produce the shoe. Somehow,
though, this all turned into a game of "warm and cold." As I
moved closer to the purloined footwear, she would yell,
"Warmer, warmer." And when I would take a step in the

wrong direction, she would correct me by saying, "Colder, colder." Fortunately, her guidance proved flawless. I found my slipper and — at the same time — met my thought for the day.

Undoubtedly, Neanderthal children played the warm and cold game. It's just a part of children. They seem to learn it without needing to be taught, like breathing. Once again, however, we see the simplest practices producing the most powerful metaphors.

When we are close to discovering something important, we become *warmer*. When we get untracked, and move away from a valuable find, we become *colder*. If the desired object is the likes of a slipper, we may not notice much change in temperature or temperament. But when we move toward certain crucial visions, we encounter a force that produces a deep feeling of warmth. And those, like Ebenezer Scrooge, who fight their callings, may best be described as cold.

In grade school I learned that people receive a "calling" that steers us toward our vocations. At first I thought it came only to those headed for the clergy. It wasn't until years passed that I understood we all have callings. In fact, I now suspect we each have very special callings.

I don't have the ability to prove the existence of a calling. It doesn't seem to be something one can capture and hand to another. Perhaps it is best to rely on a bit of time-honored wisdom borrowed from Franz Werfel's *Song of Bernadette*: "To those who believe, no explanation is necessary; to those who do not, no explanation is possible."

The relationship between courage and one's calling is

not complicated. Courage is necessary only if there is such a thing as a calling. Being true to "thine own self" means listening for and then acting upon one's calling. Nothing easy about this. It requires humility, honesty and courage. "Being me" means answering my call.

Some have described the calling as an "inner voice." Others have insisted that it comes from an external point. We must understand, however, that this does not necessarily suggest different sources. As with courage, we can connect with our callings at different times and places. Although the return address may change, the sender remains the same. If you believe that callings only resonate from one place, you greatly increase the likelihood of missing your mission in life. No one can predict where or how a calling will come.

We can distinguish dreams from callings. During the course of a lifetime we may have many dreams. Sometimes dreams fade and give way to new ones. But even those that eventually vanish have value in that they add color to a particular era of our lives. Unfulfilled dreams can even produce pleasant memories. It may, for instance, make you smile when remembering that you once hoped to have twenty children.

A calling, however, is relentless. It represents more than a creation of our changeable minds. It arrives at some point (sometimes very early) in our lives, and there it lives on doing exactly what its name implies — calling. It calls us to a particular task or set of tasks. Often people receive a series of callings, each somehow setting the stage for the next. David, for example, the physician I spoke of in Chapter Four, now feels his future may lie in writing fiction. But he does not regret the tremendous effort and sacrifice he went through during all his years of medical training. On the contrary, one path — in some way — led to the other. An aggressive and somewhat discontented doctor, he allowed his life experiences to lead him toward becoming a settled and reflective writer. He seems to be getting warmer.

We need dreams to find our callings. They start us looking beyond ourselves and into the realm of what could be. Callings have never been verified by science. Consequently, they tend to be heard more often by those courageous enough to decide for themselves what is real. I don't know this for sure, but I gather that one must be something of a dreamer to hear a calling.

"Believe that life is worth living," remarked William James, "and your belief will help create the fact." For our purposes, we can paraphrase James: "Believe you have a calling, and this belief will improve your hearing." It's hard to recognize a force you don't believe in. Even when it screams in your ear.

~~ ~~ ~~

Sometimes it screams. Sometimes it whispers. It can be easy to miss. It can be impossible to overlook. One's calling can make itself known while one touches the depths of despair or reaches the heights of ecstasy.

Just because one's calling may be obvious does not guarantee that it will be discovered. Growing up on the seashore I was reminded time and time again how people can miss the totally apparent. At least several times each summer, tourists driving along Atlantic Avenue (within a stone's throw of that great body of water) would stop and ask for directions to the ocean. It's hard to answer such a question without sounding sarcastic. I remember each time wanting to say, "Do you see that huge blue thing? That's the ocean!" But that would have been too cruel. Actually, there may be no one more embarrassed than one who realizes that he has been sitting next to the ocean and could not find it.

I suppose I have no right to be too critical. I guess we all have missed an ocean or two in our day. It's such a shame — oceans have so much to offer.

Like oceans, we can miss callings. But because we may be the only ones who can hear our callings, stopping to ask directions from bystanders may not provide all the information needed. Because we cannot rely solely on the advice of others, we need to develop a sensitivity that allows us to notice the sights, sounds and textures contained within ourselves and our world, I really believe that if those tourists had looked for the beach or simply enjoyed the scenery, instead of searching for someone to tell them where it was, they would have found it much sooner. More importantly, if you constantly hunt for others to tell you about your calling, you may miss it altogether.

Before we can go on we must consider the question, "Where do these callings come from?" Until we feel comfortable with an answer to this, we may never understand the true nature of a calling.

Several possibilities emerge. First, perhaps we are directed by our genes. Maybe our DNA contains a special set of directions, unique to each individual, that persuade us to move in particular ways. If we asked the scientific community, this theory would likely be strongly supported. After all, a biologist who is only a biologist will tend to look for biological explanations.

And this theory would seem accurate were it not for one thing. I believe I have seen people communicate with the source of these callings. They ask for guidance and clarification. Even when the answers lack absolute precision, the communication continues. Later, they return to the source to express their appreciation and gratitude. Although I know little about genes, I don't believe they are capable of dialogue.

We have to look elsewhere to find the voice that sends the calls.

A second hypothesis comes from the social sciences and is called "conditioning." This theory suggests that one can be trained to accept any path in life. For example, with the proper reinforcement, a child can be conditioned to become virtually anything from a poet to a thief. It all depends on the child's environment.

But here again we see a popular explanation with severe limitations. I believe that just about everyone in the helping professions has encountered individuals who are miserable with the lives they have been conditioned to accept. One can live out the family myth, take over the family business, receive all the reinforcers along the way and then recognize an enormous void in one's life. In other words, what one is conditioned to do may not be what one is called to do.

We can be conditioned to deny our callings but this denial will not last forever. A calling cannot be conditioned away. Even when circumstances lead us in other directions, the calling remains. Should we continue to refuse our tasks, we become colder and more discontented. Conditioning may influence our behavior, but it does not impact our callings.

So what would we find if we could trace the voice? A particular chromosome? A collection of life experiences that mold one's destiny? No. Our callings do not reach us through our senses or our psyches. They come to us through our spiritual dimensions.

These messages request that we travel paths unique to each of us. And yet our callings urge us all toward similar moral vocations. We all hear a plea to help each other. We are all, as Schweitzer pointed out, called to serve. Not everyone, however, follows this request. We have the freedom to refuse. But if we turn our backs on our callings, we become cold.

I believe that while answering our callings we find God. In fact, this may be how God likes us to find Him. Perhaps this is ultimately what a calling is all about, finding God. So I proceed with a faith that our callings come from God. Although I cannot prove this, I do know that few things provide as much courage as this faith.

Staying true to our callings requires — and produces — courage.

I wonder how much of what we call "mental illness" and "emotional disturbance" is really the consequence of repressed callings. I cannot say for certain, but I think we have grounds to believe that a great deal of the depression, anxiety and guilt present in our world comes as a result of people turning away from their special purposes.

A "people person" who spends most of her waking hours dealing with computers may never find contentment no matter how many wonderful programs she writes. Finding her road to serenity will mean finding the road where she belongs.

There are unhappy lawyers who need to be teachers just as there are melancholy teachers who need to be attorneys. There are wealthy misers who need to be generous.

There are drug addicts who need to be drug counselors. There are "takers" who are called to be "givers."

When one neglects a calling, psychological and spiritual discomfort develops. It may be a dull aching pain for a time but it can become excruciating. It can even build to the point where one can confuse the hurt with the calling.

Pamela, a divorced mother of two, told me: "I'm just one of those people who are supposed to have a bad life. You know, like it's my fate to be the bad apple." Pam gave birth to her first child at age fifteen. Now at age thirty-three and still on welfare, her sixteen-year-old daughter is six months pregnant. Soon to become a grandmother, Pam feels a powerful urge to review her situation and try to make sense of an existence that seems to her to have consisted solely of retreating from life into a long series of bad relationships with men. At this crossroads in her life, she is becoming aware that she has a calling. In her upset and confusion, however, she grasps for the most available answer. Since she has known more failure and pain than anything else, she had concluded that this must be her "fate." When she considered her purpose, she felt pain. She mistakenly took the hurt to be her destiny. She did not understand that her despair and guilt were voices urging her to change her life.

In some ways, Pam made the same mistake as modern psychology. They both suggest that our experiences, more than anything else, determine our futures. This, however, is an unfortunate myth. We can, at virtually any point in our lives, be called to take unexpected turns. These unexpected turns should not be confused with impulsive or inconsiderate changes that result from impatience, anger or immaturity. Rather, we can come to an awareness of new tasks and challenges that, after careful consideration, seem to need our special abilities. They catch our eye, then our soul.

Even if nothing in our past prepared us for such an under-taking, a drive emerges to fill this particular void. Should we turn away our eyes and our souls, we come to feel guilt, anxiety, depression or any of a number of spiritual and psychological symptoms.

People like Pam, who believe themselves to be failures, will eventually be called to make contributions. Pam may not have been a good mother but she is struggling with a grow-ing awareness that she is being called to be a good grand-mother. Inside, she feels fear. Nothing in her past has pre-pared her for such a role. Still, she is coming to understand what she needs to do. Should she heed her calling, she will find more strength than she has ever known.

If not, well . . . sadly . . . her erroneous "fate" may win out.

"To live is to suffer," wrote Viktor Frankl. "To survive is to find meaning in the suffering." Because we suffer does not mean it is our fate to live tragic lives. The pain is not the calling although the pain can point to one's mission in life. I have seen this point confirmed over and over again. Certain people cannot find their paths until they reach their darkest hours. Like Mark, the suicidal adolescent discussed in Chap-ter One, many folks find their way at the point where all seems lost.

I have become convinced of this after seeing many of my counseling clients not only survive tragedy but emerge from it with a greater sense of themselves and clearer direc-tion in their lives. I also know this from firsthand experience.

Several years ago, I had a dream come true. I received a one year appointment to the graduate faculty of a midwestern university. I had always wanted such an opportunity and although this was only a temporary position, I was promised that at the end of the year I could apply for a permanent one. I figured I had "made it."

As the first few months passed, all seemed well except for one thing — I couldn't write. For the first time ever I actually had time to sit and compose but nothing filled the space. More time went by. Still nothing. As the first semester ended, I rationalized to myself that I was going through an adjustment period and that I would soon find many new topics to write about.

Shortly into the new semester, however, I knew my problem could not be explained away so easily. I became increasingly restless and less involved with the students. I became short tempered and sarcastic and as my frustration grew, the students became more and more disappointing to me. I did not know it at the time, but they could not possibly have provided what I needed.

When my "college professor year" came to an end, I applied for the permanent position. Disenchanted with university life, I had to keep reminding myself, "This is what you've always wanted!" "Besides," I thought, "maybe writing isn't that important to you after all."

Today it seems so predictable that I would be denied the permanent position but, at the time, I was taken by complete surprise and left devastated. I had never experienced such a setback in the professional arena. I felt rejected and humiliated. I couldn't sleep for several nights and eating didn't matter much. I had lost a dream and couldn't immediately see any consolation.

In the middle of one of those sleepless nights, however, important events began to harmonize. The writers' block shattered and I found myself lost in the writing process. The feelings and the passions as well as the questions and the stories reemerged. I had to lose the dream to re-find the calling. Now I teach on a part-time basis and I love it. It has an important place in my life. But I need to do many other things.

We need to understand that we may not be masters of our missions. I believe I'm supposed to continue writing but I am also completely cognizant of the fact that there are many many individuals who write better than I. I cannot explain why someone would be called to something he or she is not particularly good at. Perhaps I will be able to in time.

Furthermore, happy endings are not guaranteed. A calling may not lead you to your preconceived notion of success. And even if it does, it may exact a tremendous toll along the way. Consider the path of Abraham Lincoln. Early in his career he tried to develop a small business but he eventually went broke. He ran for Congress twice, losing both times. He also lost two bids to become senator. Attacked daily in the press, he was despised by half the country.[1] Then, only after having his life cut short by an assassin's bullet, did the impact of his life become clear. Now he "belongs to the ages."

If we could comprehend all the things in this universe, there would be no need for faith or courage. If we wait for a calling to explain itself in complete detail before we act, we will live unfulfilled lives that end before they ever really get started.

We now have a clearer picture of the experience of tragedy. Earlier we considered the mystery of how some people emerge from suffering with a stronger sense of direction and purpose in their lives. Just when they seem headed for a breakdown, they achieve a breakthrough. Psychologically, it is unexplainable.

Yet if we understand the nature of a calling, an answer appears. Experiences that bring us closer to God also bring us closer to our callings. Few things cause us to readjust our relationship with God as much as tragedy. There are atheists who become believers and believers who become atheists. Some agnostics make choices while others grow even more agnostic. But those who move closer to God find a path. This path may not be fully prepared. It may need mowing, clearing and work of all kinds. These obstacles, however, are part of the path.

What we do with our suffering helps determine what becomes of our lives. Within every suffering soul there lies the question, "What do I do now?" Whether or not one finds an answer depends on where one goes to find it.

Sam had been an alcoholic for a long time. But this time he believed he was going to make it. He had been sober for eight weeks when he smiled and told me, "I used to do everything I could to stay out of trouble and I was always in trouble. Now that I face the music, I have fewer problems." That smile then turned to a wince as he paused and added, "Too bad it took me forty-nine years to learn that."

We may not be able to get on with our lives until we begin to face life. Furthermore, it's not until we get on with our lives that we find the rewards of courage. Paul Tillich described the rewards of courage in a single word — joy. "Joy," he said, "is the emotional expression of the courageous Yes to one's own true being."[2] But, of course, joy was Tillich's word; it may not be powerful enough, or quiet enough, for you. Courage can produce feelings as deep as feelings can go and as high as life can take us. Some may call it joy. Others may call it triumph. Still others may call it simple serenity.

Maybe every journey to courage produces a different reward. Maybe we all experience joy in our own unique ways. But we must give credit where it is due. To think only that "I survived" reflects a lack of respect and appreciation for oneself. We begin to build self-respect when we can say to ourselves, "I survived when I could easily have collapsed. I do have the gift of finding courage."

Then thank your source of courage.

No one is called to evil. No calling ever leads anyone to a destructive lifestyle. A calling asks you to contribute to the world in a unique and creative way. It is only when the calling is avoided that evil becomes possible. In his book, *Escape from Freedom*, Eric Fromm correctly observed that "the more the drive towards life is thwarted, the stronger is the drive towards destruction; the more life is realized, the less is the strength of destructiveness. Destructiveness is the outcome of an unlived life." This destructiveness includes self-destruction. Indeed all forms of destructiveness include an element of self-destructiveness.

We must then ask, "What can thwart our efforts to live our callings?" Although physical circumstances may impose obstacles, the only real barrier is a *lack of courage*. Yet when we face the fears that come with honestly living our callings, we find courage. And when we walk through these special fears, we also find our direction in life.

G.K. Chesterton saw courage as something of a contradiction. "It means a strong desire to live taking the form of a readiness to die," he claimed, voicing a sentiment that has been shared by many who have considered the subject. Finding people or causes worth dying for may represent the ultimate courage. Sacrificing one's life for one's convictions demonstrates quite clearly the power of human courage.

Not all who possess the strength of martyrs are called to be martyrs. While few of us are asked to die for our beliefs, we are all — every day of our lives — placed in situations where we are called to live for them. We are called to live our faith, our values, our beliefs. And while we live these qualities, we need to reevaluate them. Our interpretations can change as we age. Growth means change and courage means daring to act in the face of uncertainty.

And the courage that allows us to develop our beliefs is the same force that fortifies us when we feel pressured to compromise an essential value.

Consider the words of the Hasidic rabbi, Susya, who shortly before his death said, "When I get to heaven they will not ask me, 'Why were you not Moses?' Instead they will ask, 'Why were you not Susya? Why did you not become what only you could become?' "[3] He understood the need we all have to live out our special missions. When we do not carry out these missions, when we hide from our necessary tasks, "we feel ourselves guilty on account of the unused life, the unlived life in us."[4]

If, however, living your calling seems frightening, you

might be tempted to put it off until that big "someday" down the road. And if we were guaranteed that our lives would reach beyond that distant someday, this defense might be comforting. But as mortal beings we can be called from this life at any time. We all, at some level, know this. Putting important tasks off until someday does not ease guilt or build security. It only generates feelings of cowardice.

The presence of death adds urgency to our callings. We know that we do not have forever to do what we need to do. We feel the firm yet gentle push to contribute what only we can contribute. In the end, being true to yourself means that you made an honest and courageous effort to answer your call.

Furthermore, I suspect that those who insulate themselves most thoroughly from death have the most difficult time finding their purposes in life. It is during moments when we are reminded of our mortality that our missions seem clearest. When we answer the question, "If I died today, what would I regret most about my life?" we are pointed in the direction of what we need to do. Consequently, people who live with stockpiles of medicine and bandages, locked behind walls that never allow anything in but the sterile, the routine and the ordinary are the ones most likely to feel lost and aimless.

Did you ever wonder why in every picture of the Grim Reaper, he is always pointing that bony finger at something? An awareness of death points us toward valuable lessons. Sometimes we have to meet the fear to learn the lesson.

When you walk through a fear, you walk to courage, a courage that will stay with you and can be used again and again. When you reach the other side of fear, you will also encounter other treasures. You may find a certain kind of peace, a sense of accomplishment, a feeling of triumph, and some wisdom.

Plato described courage as "knowing what not to fear," pointing to the link between courage and wisdom. More specifically, it speaks of the valor that accompanies a sense of purpose. A soul with a mission recognizes fear but will not let it interfere with the task at hand. Fear did not stop Schweitzer or Lincoln. They knew their missions were vastly more important than the risks involved.

Just as marathon runners feel less pain as they come into sight of their destinations, we are less likely to feel the strains and pains of failures if we keep at least one eye on our ultimate goals.

The idea of running into a burning building may be terrifying. But if you had a loved one trapped inside, you might not give it a second thought before rushing in. Likewise, if you find fulfillment through helping the homeless, you probably won't be too discouraged should someone call you foolish or quixotic. Nor will you be too upset should one of your beneficiaries complain that the blanket you gave him is not the right color. When you believe in what you do, the slings and arrows of outrageous fortune lose a lot of their sting.

Honorable goals have a way of eliminating fears. Fears gain power as we dwell on them. If we keep our attention pointed toward living out our tasks, we will not be imprisoned by threats of criticism and discomfort. As we respond to our callings, we learn what not to fear.

All callings have equal value. The housewife's mission is every bit as venerable as that of a Supreme Court justice.

The old man who builds a garden is just as necessary as the young man who builds a skyscraper. All our missions are essential. During the course of our lifetimes we may not see all the consequences of our efforts. Ants never get to see how intricate their farms are and they probably never come to understand how the entire system depends on their individual efforts. In order to comprehend the ant organization, we must look at it from above. It's difficult to get such a perspective on the human world.

We say that animals and insects are guided by nature. (Isn't it interesting that no one ever questions the existence of nature? I've never heard anyone suggest that nature does not exist or that it is dead. And we never ask nature to produce miracles to prove its existence.) Well, we too are guided. But it can be hard to see how the pieces fit. More importantly, we are not in a position to scorn anyone's contribution. I don't pretend to know how all the pieces fit. But it's my hunch they all fit together better when they respect each other.

We are all pieces, and only pieces. We are all important pieces.

We now find ourselves approaching the end of this exploration. The temptation exists to add more words, cover all the bases, anticipate all the questions. But I promised to keep this experience a simple one. After all, courage can be lost in words.

Courage exists, always. We need not ask, "Is it there?" Instead, the appropriate question is, "How do I reach it?" Courage remains even when we lose contact with it. In order to tap it, we must hold on to this simple fact.

Karl Jaspers once said, "What man is, he has become through that cause which he has made his own." A person's "cause" can be anything from working to place a human on Mars to trying to be kind and generous throughout one's life. It is only when we become aware of our cause that we begin a genuine search for courage. Prior to this point in our lives, we only need it to get us through the challenges we cannot avoid.

Once we become aware of our callings, our needs change. We then need courage not only to respond to life, but also to *prepare for life*. Answering a call means stating, "I want to live my life courageously." It is precisely at this point that we come to really understand our need for courage.

Courage is more available to us if we are on the right path, the path we have been called to travel. Even here, however, it can be a struggle to discover. It can take effort and determination. Because we all receive a calling to help others, behaviors such as kindness and generosity tend to instill strength in us all. This much seems guaranteed. But courage exists that can only be reached through our unique journeys. Thus we share certain avenues to courage and we each find and build avenues of our own.

But this much I can promise. If you stay on your path and remain true to your calling, then, even if you cannot find courage, courage will find you.

Honor your calling.

If I had more courage I would

Norm, what will you do with
what you have learned?

# Drs. Casey, Goldman, Lischwe, & Garrett, P.L.C.

*Catherine S. Casey, M.D., William D. Goldman, M.D.*
*Catherine A. Lischwe, M.D., Mary G. Garrett, M.D., Nancy C. Kim, M.D.*

1715 N. George Mason Drive, Suite 205, Arlington, Virginia 22205
Phone: 703/522-7300    Fax: 703/522-0495

*Practice limited to children and adolescents*

**Directions:**

We receive courage from others,
and we can provide courage to
others

"Being there for one other person"

people provide courage
what encourages me?
self-respect reminds that you're following
a path of courage

# References

## Chapter I

1. Bettelheim, B. (1977), *The Uses of Enchantment*, Vintage Books Edition, p. 8.
2. Ibid., p. 122.
3. May, R. (1976), *The Courage to Create*, Bantam Edition.
4. Franklin, B. (1973), *The Autobiography*, New York: Collier.

## Chapter II

1. Prather, H. (1976), *Notes to Myself*, Bantam Books.
2. "How Dr. Suess Battles Pain With Whimsy," in *St. Louis Post-Dispatch*, October 22, 1986.
3. Henderson, B. (1986), *Rotten Reviews*, Pushcart Press, p. 33.
4. Ibid., p. 33.
5. Ibid., p. 16.
6. Henderson, B. (1987), *Rotten Reviews II*, Pushcart Press, p. 87.
7. Ibid., p. 17.
8. In Safire, W. & Safire, L. (Eds.), *Words of Wisdom: More Good Advice*, Simon and Schuster, 1989, p. 102.
9. Gourgey, C., "Integrity and Self-Esteem," *P.A.G.L. Newsletter*, September, 1985, p. 5.
10. Zimbardo, P.G. (1977), *Shyness*, Jove, p. 23.
11. Ibid., p. 25.
12. May, R. (1985), *My Quest for Beauty*, Saybrook, p. 22.
13. Andrews, L. M. (1987), *To Thine Own Self Be True*, New York: Anchor Press/Doubleday, p. 170.
14. Kennedy, J.F. (1964), *Profiles in Courage*, Harper and Row, pp. 209-210.

## Chapter III

1. Servan-Schreiber, J. (1987), *The Return of Courage*, Addison-Wesley Publishing Co., Inc., p. 3.

2. Siegel, B.S. (1989), *Peace, Love and Healing*, Harper and Row, p. 193.
3. Maslow, A. (1971), *The Farther Reaches of Human Nature*, Penguin Books, p. 37.
4. Canavan, D. (1989), "Fear of Success," in R. C. Curtis (Ed.) *Self-defeating Behaviors*, New York: Plenum Press, pp. 159-188.

### Chapter IV

1. Hoff, B. (1982), *The Tao of Pooh*, Penguin Books, pp. 64-65.
2. Buscaglia, L. (1978), *Personhood*, Charles B. Slack, Inc., p. 21.
3. Maslow, A. (1971), *The Farther Reaches of Human Nature*, Penguin Books, pp. 34-35.
4. Taylor, S.E. (1989), *Positive Illusions*, New York: Basic Books, Inc.
5. Lazarus, R.S. (November, 1979), "Positive Denial: The Case for Not Facing Reality," *Psychology Today*.
6. In Milsten, D.R. (1987), *Will Rogers: The Cherokee Kid*, Glenheath Publishers.

### Chapter V

1. Ansbacher, H.L. & Ansbacher, R.R. (1956), *The Individual Psychology of Alfred Adler*, Basic Books, Inc.
2. Fabry, J.B. (1980), *The Pursuit of Meaning* (2nd ed.), Harper and Row.
3. de Mello, A. (1982), *The Song of the Bird*, Image Books.
4. May, R. (1975), *The Courage to Create*, W. W. Norton and Co.
5. Taylor, S.E. (1989), *Positive Illusions*, Basic Books, Inc.
6. Minuchin, S. (1974), *Families and Family Therapy*, Harvard University Press.

### Chapter VI

1. "This Will Make You Feel Better" (1986), United Technologies Corporation, Hartford, Connecticut.
2. Tillich, P. (1952), *The Courage To Be*, Yale University Press.
3. M. Friedman, Introduction to M. Buber, *Between Man and Man*, New York: Macmillan, 1965, p. xix.
4. Rank, O. (1945), *Will Therapy and Truth and Reality*, New York: Alfred A. Knopf.